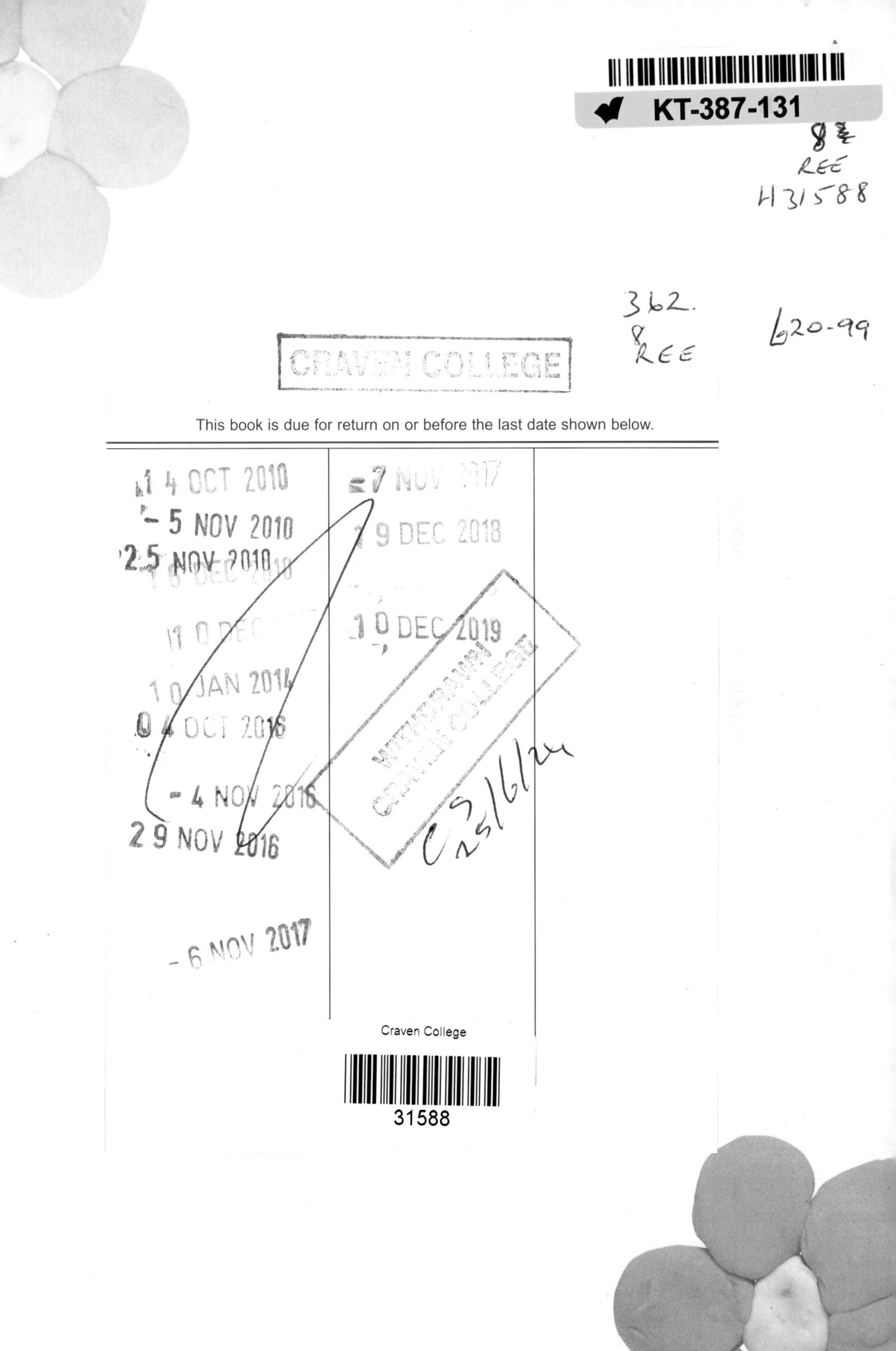

Reflective Practice in the Early Years

Edited by
Michael Reed and Natalie Canning

Los Angeles | London | New Delhi
Singapore | Washington DC

First published 2010

SAGE Publications Ltd
1 Oliver's Yard
55 City Road
London EC1Y 1SP

SAGE Publications Inc.
2455 Teller Road
Thousand Oaks, California 91320

SAGE Publications India Pvt Ltd
B 1/I 1 Mohan Cooperative Industrial Area
Mathura Road
New Delhi 110 044

SAGE Publications Asia-Pacific Pte Ltd
33 Pekin Street #02-01
Far East Square
Singapore 048763

Library of Congress Control Number: 2009924600

British Library Cataloguing in Publication data

A catalogue record for this book is available from the British Library

ISBN 978-1-84860-161-1
ISBN 978-1-84860-162-8 (pbk)

Typeset by C&M Digitals (P) Ltd, Chennai, India
Printed in Great Britain by MPG Group, Bodmin, Cornwall
Printed on paper from sustainable resources

For Tess and children everywhere

Contents

List of Figures

About the Editors and Contributors

Editors

Michael Reed's career has involved senior positions in schools, developing and managing a large day nursery, and running a training and development consultancy. He has worked on projects for the Open University forming part of the course development and writing team for the Foundation Degree and has written for a number of publications. He teaches on a range of undergraduate and postgraduate early years programmes at the University of Worcester as part of the Centre for Early Childhood tutorial team.

Natalie Canning is Lecturer in Education – Early Years at the Open University. Her background is in playwork and social work, particularly supporting children to explore their personal, social and emotional issues through play. She has undertaken research in the area of children's empowerment in play and is currently involved in research on developing children as autonomous learners. She has previously worked at the University College Plymouth, St Mark and St John as the Programme Leader for the Foundation Degree in Early Years (Child Development) and has taught across a variety of Early Childhood undergraduate and postgraduate programmes.

Contributors

Mandy Andrews is a Senior Lecturer at the University of Worcester in the Centre for Early Childhood within the Institute of Education. She teaches on Early Years Professional Status routes and undergraduate and postgraduate modules in Early Childhood. She was formerly

Project Director of a large Sure Start Local Programme and Children's Centre in Cornwall. Her research interests include leadership and children's play and empowerment.

Karen Appleby has a professional heritage in early years teaching. She is a Senior Lecturer in Early Childhood and Learning and Teaching Fellow at the University of Worcester. She is Partnership Co-ordinator for the Centre for Early Childhood, in the Institute of Education, and teaches across a variety of Early Childhood programmes. Previously she has worked as the Course Leader for the BA (Hons) Integrated Early Childhood Studies and HND in Early Childhood Studies.

Sue Baylis became a tutor with the Pre-School Learning Alliance and trained as a Specialist Teaching Assistant. After gaining a degree in Early Childhood she moved into special education working in a Nursery Assessment Unit attached to a special school. Following postgraduate studies in inclusive and special education she became a tutor for autism.west midlands and is now a Senior Lecturer at the University of Worcester where she is engaged in research into the inclusion of children with ASD.

Sue Callan is a Senior Lecturer in the Centre for Early Childhood at the University of Worcester. Sue works with students on the Sector Endorsed Foundation Degree in Early Years (SEFDEY), BA (Hons) Early Childhood Studies and assesses on the Early Years Professional Status programme. She coordinates the delivery of courses with partner institutions, including a local authority children's service and is also an Associate Lecturer of the Open University. She is a contributor to *Mentoring in the Early Years* and co-editor of *Managing Early Years Settings – Leading and Supporting Teams,* both published by Sage.

Victoria Cooper is a Senior Lecturer with the Open University. She teaches across a range of undergraduate early years, educational research, health, and social care programmes. She is joint course chair for the Certificate in Early Years Practice and course chair for the postgraduate module in Child Development. Her background is as an early years teacher, research psychologist and a lecturer in further and higher education. Her research interests include children's identity, mental health and the education of young people.

Kate Fowler has spent time teaching within a variety of early years settings. She is a Senior Lecturer in the Centre for Early Childhood at the University of Worcester. She teaches on undergraduate and postgraduate Early Childhood programmes and is the FdA Early Childhood coordinator for three partner colleges in the West Midlands. She has undertaken research in the areas of reflective practice, partnership and mentoring relationships and the development of creativity in practitioners in order to facilitate and nurture the child's general well-being and development.

Alison Jackson is an early years practitioner with over 20 years experience working with children under eight in a range of settings. She has been a Nursery Supervisor and is an accredited Childminder. Her experience has included acting as Chair of a pre-school management committee and Chair of her county Childminding Association. She is a member of her local Early Years and Extended Services Forum and an early years representative on the local Schools Forum. Alison has completed a Foundation Degree in Early Years and is currently studying for a BA (Hons) in Integrated Early Childhood Studies and is working towards Early Years Professional Status.

Rory McDowall Clark originally trained as a nursery and primary teacher. She has had a wide range of experience in broader social contexts including community development with charities and voluntary organisations and outreach youth work. Rory worked as an educational consultant for a number of local authorities before taking up a post in the Centre for Early Childhood at the University of Worcester where she has been a Senior Lecturer for the past 10 years. Her research interests include gender, cultural views of the child and continuing professional development.

Wendy Messenger has held senior positions in schools. She is now a Senior Lecturer at the University of Worcester and course leader for the Postgraduate Certificate in Integrated Children's Services. She teaches across a variety of programmes at undergraduate and postgraduate level. Her interests include early years education, inclusion and multi-agency working. Her research interests include professional cultures, collaborative working and multi-professional training. She is currently undertaking research in these areas with reference to Children's Centres in the UK.

Alison Morrall has worked with families and children in various contexts. She has over 25 years experience working in the field of education and early years provision and is a contributor to *Mentoring* *in the Early Years* book published by Sage. She tutors for the Learning Skills Council in Hereford and is currently delivering training to early years practitioners on language and play programmes. She is completing postgraduate studies in Educational Management and Leadership and works as a visiting lecturer at the University of Worcester.

Claire Majella Richards is Senior Lecturer and Course Leader for the Integrated Early Childhood Studies Degree within the Institute of Education at the University of Worcester. She has extensive experience of multi-agency partnership working having been employed within the voluntary and statutory sectors. Her roles have varied in the fields of mental health nursing, substance misuse services and lately with the social concern of domestic abuse. As a qualified barrister, she remains a committed advocate to the rights of children and is engaged with the activities of the local Safeguarding Children Board.

Linda Tyler is a Senior Lecturer at the University of Worcester in the Centre for Early Childhood. Previously she has worked as a teacher and coordinator for ICT, Literacy and Science in a BECTa award-winning school. She has designed and delivered ICT training for a local authority and developed several ICTogether groups to enhance parent ICT skills working with parents and children. She is researching the effects of Podcasting on children's communication skills in order to develop a Teacher Training package for students. She has published work online about the use of Avatars as a medium for improving literacy.

Rosie Walker is currently a Children's Centre Manager of a cluster of two phase 1 Children's Centres and is leading the transition from an Early Years Centre to Children's Centre. She is an Associate Tutor on the National Professional Qualification for Integrated Centre Leadership programme. She is trained as a Social Worker and worked in a variety of voluntary and statutory settings in childcare. These include Child Guidance, NSPCC and Child Protection Training. She set up a Family Support Service in 1997 and acted as a mentor for post-qualifying Social Work students. Rosie has been a visiting lecturer at universities throughout the South West and the Midlands.

Acknowledgements

The editors would like to acknowledge the work of all contributors to the text and the practitioners who have provided insights to practice, particularly the Powys Foundation Phase Team and the Senior Management Team, staff and parents at the Children's Centre involved in the research for Chapter 8. We would also like to acknowledge the student contributions from the University of Worcester, the Open University and the University College Plymouth, St Mark and St John. Thanks must finally go to Jude Bowen and Amy Jarrold at Sage Publications for their support and assistance throughout this project.

Introduction

Michael Reed and Natalie Canning

Reflecting on practice underpins the work of an early years practitioner. This is quite a bold statement, considering a practitioner needs to provide opportunities for children to learn and make sense of the world. They have to do this by developing an enabling environment; work in partnership with parents, protect children, understand a raft of policy initiatives and plan to meet the demands of an early years curriculum. So why is reflection so important? In simple terms, it is because all of these initiatives, developments, policies and practices have to be thought about, tested, considered, and delivered in practice. In effect, without reflection on practice we are left with only a functional mechanism to improve knowledge, to consider new initiatives, define and refine practice and to respond to change. There is now a clear expectation for early years practitioners to carefully consider and reflect upon the way they engage with children and families. Indeed, it could be said that reflecting on practice is now an essential part of a practitioner's role in the 21st century. We say this not because of Government directives or because a Government agency thinks this will enhance the practice of the workforce. We say it because this is what practitioners are showing they are more than capable of doing. It is our contention that practitioners have active and lively minds, and not solely technocrats who gain skills and competencies. They have a basic disposition to make sense of experience, investigate it, care about others, relate to children and adapt to their physical and cultural environment. What is more, they can engage with others, compare, contrast and deepen their understanding if encouraged to do so.

As for whether commentators can universally agree upon ways to define and encourage 'reflection' is another matter. There has appeared over the last few years a range of opinions and research evidence that underlines the importance of reflection. These have encompassed not only the field of education, but law, music, theatre and the medical profession. Much of the evidence surrounding the origins and ongoing debates about the nature of professional reflection is contained in this book. However, a few examples may be useful. Moon (2008) sees reflection as a set of abilities and skills and developing ways to take a critical stance. Brookfield (1995) suggests that learners are reflecting when they offer analysis about personal experiences. Schön (1983) speaks of reflective practitioners who are thoughtful and contemplative and use intuition, insight and artistry. Perhaps this tells us about the need to see reflection as an emotional response that complements our knowledge and what we understand about a subject. It enables us to consider how we act and might act in a situation. In essence, reflection can be described as a means of helping those most closely involved to think about what they already know and consider ways they might want to improve or refine a situation. This may involve gaining more insight or knowledge about what goes on, which may well determine other ways to refine and develop their actions or relationships with others. Reflection is also important in a time of change. It allows us to consider ourselves and the changing world, to explore options and come to terms with new ideas and changing roles, responsibilities and relationships. Reflection provides us with a framework in order to manage our perceptions of the world around us. This is particularly important today when one of the few certainties within the early years sector is that change is occurring and is certain to occur in the future.

Different chapters of the book describe the way practitioners are responding to change and reflecting on practice. The practitioners represented in the chapters come from a range of different backgrounds, and from all over the UK. Their experiences are explored through the contexts of training, managing childcare settings, delivering the curriculum, experiencing the impact of policy decisions and working collaboratively. The book is organised into four sections which are loosely based on the four principles of the Early Years Foundation Stage, but which also reflect key issues for early years practitioners. Each chapter contributes a different perspective to the overall theme of the section, for example, in Section 1, 'Children's Learning and Development', you will encounter not only practical ways in which practitioners support children's learning and development, but why reflective practice is essential to developing professionalism. We explore the nature of reflection and the ways that reflection on practice can enhance self-awareness and contribute to professional development. Key themes of this section include understanding different ways of working to explore how practitioners work with and interpret key legislative developments. More importantly, this section considers why it is important to be reflective and the subsequent impact this has on children in our care. The second section, 'The Unique Child', builds on these themes and addresses two significant areas of early years practice, understanding how we work towards providing opportunities for healthy children and ways in which we work to safeguard them. These chapters focus on the implications for the child at the centre of the process. They consider different perspectives of practitioners and how reflective thinking can support children's individual needs. We then move on to consider how reflective practice supports 'Enabling Professional Environments'. This section looks at the way in which early years professionals come together to support the development of children, families and communities. The chapters here emphasise the changing nature of early years practice, the way in which it is organised and the move towards multi-agency working and sharing professional expertise. Nevertheless, positive environments are unable to be facilitated without building on positive professional relationships, and Section 4, 'Positive Relationships in a Multi-agency World' provides examples of different ways in which practitioners are working towards developing these. Different perspectives are considered in how we develop, support and maintain communities of practice, and this final section looks at the different ways early years professionals are undertaking this challenge and how they have developed critical reflection skills on their personal learning journey.

Being reflective helps us to consider what motivates practitioners to understand their individual and collective roles, responsibilities, and relationships. Importantly, how these can be adapted and even change. We can do this by listening to the views of others, understand what has motivated them to change and in the process probably recognise some of ourselves as well. When their voices emanate from a realistic context that we recognise and understand, then reflection is not only useful but an essential component of working in the early years. We hope in the book we have provided some of those voices and that they will help you to consider your response to change. This you will find is a recurring theme as you move through the book and each chapter considers a different early years context. Some may be of more immediate interest than others and we are not suggesting that you start from the first page and work carefully to the end. You may care to start with the most familiar, but try to move forwards and tackle chapters that will expand your ideas and knowledge. All of the authors have a realistic and positive view of early years education;

they offer differing perspectives and within these sometimes similar interpretations. For example, the chapters on student learning tell us that students who are engaged in distance learning share some of the same apprehensions and capabilities as those following a more traditional academic route. In the same way, all the chapters reinforce the view that reflection on practice is important even though they each consider varied professional practice. As to whether the chapters represent best practice, provide a reasoned debate or just makes you think about your own practice is open to personal interpretation. There is no obligation to agree with the views expressed or to see the ideas about practice as something you must have in place. To do that would be presumptuous and undermine the whole idea of reflecting on practice. Therefore, use each of the chapters to inform your knowledge about differing aspects of early years education. It is important for you to engage in reflection as you meet parts of each chapter that ask you to reflect and use the list of references to delve into reports and find out the views of other commentators.

Finally, you may be an undergraduate student, a practitioner engaged in further study, perhaps aspiring to Early Years Professional Status. You might also (and just as importantly) be a motivated and capable practitioner who thinks that reflecting on practice actually benefits you and ultimately the children in your care. Whichever of these 'new professionals' you represent, do try and read the chapters with an open mind, and most importantly, discuss the content with other students, practitioners and tutors. In this way we will have made a start in promoting reflection on practice.

References

Brookfield, S. (1995) *Becoming a Critically Reflective Teacher*. San Francisco: Jossey-Bass.

Moon, J. (2008) *Critical Thinking: An Exploration of Theory and Practice*. London: Routledge.

Schön, D. (1983) *The Reflective Practitioner. How Professionals Think in Action.* New York: Basic Books.

Section 1

Children's Learning and Development

1

Reflective Thinking; Reflective Practice

Karen Appleby

Chapter objectives

This chapter examines reflective thinking and practice from the perspective of developing early childhood professionals who are active participants in the process of exploring and developing their own 'professional identity' and expertise as reflective practitioners. Key themes are that this process should be personally meaningful and purposeful; that it involves practitioners developing not only key values, qualities, knowledge and skills, but that it also requires the ability to articulate and represent these for themselves and for others. The examination and sharing of personal learning journeys is seen as being central to our developing understanding of 'who we are' as reflective practitioners and supporting our understanding of others. It reinforces the notion that the journey will continue. The term 'reflective practitioner' here is applied to all early child professionals, regardless of their role and is not perceived as being limited solely to those working directly with young children. As a lecturer in Early Childhood I see myself as a member of this group; consequently this chapter represents my personal interpretation of the role at the time of writing, constructed through my own experiences, the 'voices' and pictures of practice of students and colleagues in relation to wider reading.

A picture of practice: setting the scene

Current policy on workforce development embraces the principle that reflective practice is an essential tool within the *Every Child Matters: Change for Children* agenda. Bertram and Owen (2007: online) describe quality settings as being 'characterised by staff who are reflective, committed and seeking to "improve on their previous best"'. The *Common Core of Skills and Knowledge* (DfES, 2005), The *Early Years Foundation Stage* (DCSF, 2008) and *Standards for Early Years Professional Status* (EYPS) (CWDC, 2008) include the ability to apply knowledge and experience to reflect upon, think about and improve practice. Clearly reflective practice is seen as having the potential to make a difference for children and their families, as being significant for the way we respond to children and their needs. The challenge for practitioners and those supporting their professional development is how this can be achieved.

Point for reflection

Much has been written about reflective practice resulting in a confusing plethora of interpretations, associated terminology and models. Brookfield (1995: 7) suggested some years ago that one reason for the concept's popularity is the 'malleability in its meaning'. As you engage with the 'process of becoming' an effective reflective practitioner, consider these key questions:

- Why is reflection relevant to me and my practice?
- What is it?
- What does it look like?
- How do I do it?
- What are the benefits?

In seeking answers to these questions there are inherent dangers: firstly, that there is only one answer and, secondly, that someone else knows the answers and can tell you what they are. The ability to think critically and creatively about reflective practice and the confidence and motivation to construct a personal interpretation of what it means for us as individuals in our particular context, is essential to our role as reflective practitioners. This does not mean that we should ignore different perspectives; to further personal understanding it is essential that we engage with and discuss these with others. Through what Brookfield (1995) describes as 'critical reflective thinking' it is possible to examine the personal, social and political 'assumptions' surrounding what it means to be a reflective practitioner and to reach a position where we as individuals are able to make informed decisions about our practice. He presents a useful model for achieving this through the use of four 'critically reflective lenses' (Brookfield, 1995: 29–39). The principle of looking at any aspect of our practice in relation to our own autobiographies, the 'eyes' of those we are working for, our colleagues' perspectives and theoretical literature is relevant to all of us working within the profession.

Why is it important for us all to adopt a critical stance? Moss (2008: xvi) provides some insight into this when warning us against a narrow interpretation of reflective practice, one that reduces it to the role of a tool for 'governing early childhood educators' or for 'assessing one's own conformity to externally imposed norms'. He also warns us about the dangers of a mechanistic approach to reflective practice and introduces the notion of the 'reflective professional practitioner in marked contrast to the worker-as-technician' (Moss, 2008: xiii). From this perspective, it is not merely a systematic process of acquiring knowledge and skills from 'experts' and using their theories or 'models' to reflect on practice and make changes. These models provide a common reference point for examining thinking and practice but do not include the application in practice which gives them real-life meaning and purpose. They do not consider the role of the individual, or group of individuals who are exploring the relationship between theory and practice, the 'praxis' (Penney and Warelow, 1999) from which personal theories about reflective practice develop and the 'emotional tolerance' (Claxton, 2003: 2) required. These and many other factors inform the development of an individual's 'identity' as a reflective practitioner. Reflective practice is in this sense a never-ending 'learning journey' involving personal and professional qualities and attributes that merge as the individual assumes ownership of thinking processes and actions and develops a personal sense of responsibility for the 'outcomes for children' as individuals and as part of a 'community of practice' (Wenger, 1998). Rather than a 'technician' or apprentice reliant on 'unreflective induction' (Claxton, 2003: 2), the practitioner is perceived here as an 'artist' and reflective practice as an art (Schön, 1987), a creative process applied and developed in collaboration with others. With this in mind, the imposition of a strict framework that does not value diversity within the workforce or allow for different approaches and ways of experiencing the learning journey could limit the development of effective working communities and consequently the outcomes for children.

The 'voices' of those engaged in the process of becoming reflective practitioners provide individual insights into the process, challenges and benefits involved. Their first-hand experience of applying principles in practice, their responses and interpretation of experience provide other practitioners with a genuine insight into reflective practice in action. Moss's (2008: xiii) definition of reflective practice as 'a rigorous process of meaning-making, a continuous process of constructing theories of the world, testing them through dialogue and listening, then reconstructing those theories' is clearly linked with the Reggio Emilia 'pedagogy of listening' (Rinaldi, 2005). Reflective practice as an integral part of professional identity develops most effectively within a culture or learning community where individuals are actively listening and responding to the thoughts and experiences of others. This principle has relevance for anyone working within the early childhood profession, including those leading practice in early years settings such as Early Years Professionals (EYPs) and lecturers in further and higher education. Sharing thoughts and experiences supports the process of making what we know and understand explicit to ourselves as well as to others. This in turn enables us to make sense of experience and practice, to 'play' with ideas and new ways of working. This is what makes reflective practice exciting but also challenging; it involves not only thinking critically about our practice, it is also a creative, open-ended process with many potential interpretations. You can engage in this process on your own, but involve others and the possibilities are endless. This demonstrates its value as an essential element within the concept of lifelong learning and ongoing professional development.

What is involved in being a reflective practitioner?

One of the challenges for developing reflective professionals is in understanding what is involved. From a personal perspective some key themes or processes have emerged:

- **reflection** as a generic term to describe behaviours involving feeling and thinking about thoughts and experiences, in order to identify issues and to develop new understandings and insight;

- **reflective learning** implying a 'sense of open exploration' in order to find out how something is or to find out more about it (Moon, 2008: 26). Askew and Carnell (1998) examine the value of learning through action;

- **reflective thinking** that implies there is a purpose, either consciously or subconsciously. It can include critical thinking that is 'active and deliberate' (Moon, 2008: 26), creative thinking, reflection in action and on action (Schön, 1983, 1987), reflexivity or 'focusing close attention upon one's own actions' and the way 'I am experienced and perceived by others' (Bolton, 2005: 10);

- **reflective writing** as one mode of reflective thinking, expression and representation and stimulus for further reflective thinking;

- **reflective action** which informs and is informed by the other processes;

- **meta-reflection** which involves making the process of reflection explicit – reflection on reflection (Julie Davies – student comment, 2008).

Your themes and definitions may be different to these: mine are likely to have changed over time, but that is the point I am making. Do any of us have the definitive answer?

Developing a professional identity: the voices of professional practitioners

The 'voices' that follow represent some of the thoughts and experiences of a diverse group of students of different ages, academic backgrounds, experience in practice and professional roles. The insights gained from individual learning journeys are intended to stimulate questions, thoughts and discussion about the subject, and through this support others in articulating their own thinking and practice. They have provided me with a valuable 'lens' through which I have developed my personal 'voice' as a reflective practitioner (as represented within this chapter). I have also drawn on the perspectives of colleagues who are continually exploring the issue of how we nurture effective reflective practitioners. All of the issues examined in this chapter apply as much to the tutors involved as to the students.

The course

All of the 'voices' in this chapter come from students on a distinct one-year BA (Hons) Integrated Early Childhood Studies 'top-up' programme which focuses on the development of students as early childhood professionals, some of whom are or will be practitioners working directly with children and their families. The programme provides a framework for development through core modules that focus on reflective thinking and practice within the context of academic evidence and professional concerns. The learning, teaching and assessment approach is designed to support students' experience of reflective practice and the examination of their identity and learning journey as reflective practitioners within the context of the wider profession. Optional modules provide students with the opportunity to explore aspects of early childhood most relevant to them and their future careers.

Personal ownership and 'identity'

Bolton (2005: xviii), encourages us to 'fly', to 'see how it can be done if you just let go' (Turner, cited in Bolton, 2005: xviii). Personal ownership of the processes involved in being a reflective practitioner can empower us to makes best use of our individual strengths, our personal qualities and attributes. Recognising that reflective practice not only allows you to use what you know and can do but actually requires you to develop your own 'voice' can be a liberating experience. If this is to happen it is essential that reflective practice is owned predominantly by the professional practitioners involved, rather than theorists or policy makers.

Point for reflection

- What aspects of your practice give you a sense of empowerment?
- Are you conscious that you reflect on your practice and how that thinking informs what you do in similar future situations?
- Can you recognise your own strengths, personal qualities and attributes?
- Do your colleagues recognise the same or different skills?
- Do you feel you have a 'voice'?

Although it is possible to identify and label features of reflective thinking and practice in relation to theory, policy and examples from practice, it is only when we have internalised the evidence and formed our interpretation of the purpose and the process, that it becomes integral to our personal and professional identity. Julie Davis (3rd year student) labelled this process of reflecting on reflection as 'meta-reflection':

> It is the process of examining one's own reflections (reflecting back on past reflections I suppose) and really thinking about and picking to bits the reflective process you have gone through and articulating this in order to reach a deeper understanding of the process itself and how it has enabled (or otherwise!) your ability/capacity to reflect. I think that by engaging in this 'meta-reflection' you are more able to identify future opportunities for reflection (i.e. transfer the skill beyond the immediate experience) and appreciate what a powerful and empowering tool you have at your disposal!

Knowing ourselves

Ownership of the reflective process through 'meta-reflection' involves defining, evaluating and redefining our individual professional 'identity' as reflective thinkers and practitioners. Articulating our thoughts about what being reflective involves and why it is necessary to our practice, how understanding has evolved and identifying what reflective thinking and practice means to us personally and professionally, are all part of the learning process, of 'knowing ourselves'.

> Being reflective involves critically analysing your own practice and looking at what is good and what needs improving. This enables you to be able to set personal targets and to improve future practice. (Nikki Jones)

> It involves me in being honest about my practice and how and why I do things the way I do ... I am now more open to changing my thoughts and views about things. (Kelly Hampton)

> It has encouraged me to be more positive in bringing about change in my setting, to improve the quality. (Vicki Page)

Learning journeys

Recognising and valuing the learning journey and significant changes in our thoughts, values and attitudes helps us to define who we are now as well as to recognise that we will continue to change and evolve as reflective practitioners. Learning how to express and record our thoughts is essential to the 'rigorous process of meaning-making'

(Moss, 2008: xiii) and to developing confidence in our identity, for ourselves and for others, whether they are colleagues in the workplace or external bodies such as Ofsted.

> I think I understand now the process of reflection: some of this I did before (intuitively, instinctively, sub-consciously), but having an informed awareness of this has strengthened its value to me and my ability to reflect effectively. Being reflective to me is about really thinking about what I'm doing – while I'm doing it and after I've done it. The focus of my reflection is generally to improve what I'm doing and is generally related to my overarching aims, which is to improve the lives of young children – it is essentially what I am about – it helps to keep my reflection positive and productive. This gives it value to me. (Julie Davis)

Here Julie identifies a clear purpose for her reflection and the role of reflective thinking within this – her definition represents the merging of her personal perspectives with her professional identities (Clough and Corbett, 2000). Establishing a personal rationale for engaging in reflective practice enables her to self-evaluate and to use reflective thinking as a constructive process. She emphasises the importance of thinking about her actions, 'reflecting-in-action' and 'reflecting-on-action' (Schön, 1983, 1987).

The reflective process

In the following example Kim reflects on how her understanding of the reflective process developed from re-visiting an experience into a deeper appreciation of its potential for personal learning and improving practice. Action, in the view of Askew and Carnell (1998), is essential to the learning process.

> I used to think it was just about thinking over what I had done – thinking about things that had happened, but with no real result or action following the reflective process. Now I know how effective it can be in improving practice and actually changing what I think, say and do at work. It's not just about grand, massive revelations – it's the small everyday points that matter too. The small changes can make a massive difference to children!

Kim's belief in the value of reflective practice has developed from personal experience; she has 'seen' the difference it can make to children. Her sense of responsibility for the children's well-being is evident and consequently she is motivated to learn more about the processes involved, to deepen her understanding in order to improve her practice further. Brookfield's (1995) 'autobiographical lens' is a useful tool for examining assumptions and supporting a deeper level of critical thinking.

> In making effective changes to practice, we need to look at ourselves objectively and reflect upon our own values and principles with an open mind. Through my professional development, the knowledge that I have acquired has led me to question why I hold the values that I do and where they stem from ... Through engaging with my memories and the emotions attached to them I have a much clearer picture of who I am ... Through my greater self-awareness I am now able to see how my views and values influence my practice and those around me. (Alice Barnett)

Here Alice demonstrates qualities associated with the 'reflexive-minded practitioner' which Bolton (2005) defines as 'focusing close attention upon one's own actions, thoughts, feelings, values, identity and their effect upon others, situations and professional and social structures' (Bolton, 2005: 10).

Developing your identity as a reflective professional practitioner – commitment to personal change

Developing your identity as a reflective professional practitioner who aspires to be more than a 'worker-as-technician' (Moss, 2008: xiii) requires commitment as an 'agent' of personal change and recognition of your role and responsibility as a learner as well as a practitioner ...

> Taking a step back to think critically, to evaluate my experiences in order to engage in a process of life-long learning and conscious change as a professional based on informed and ethical experiences. (Shanna Bradley)

This commitment includes developing and maintaining a questioning approach where ...

> The most important thing is that you explore 'why'. Often this in turn supports change. (Permjit Tanda)

> It's not just looking at *what* you did, it's thinking about *why* you did it; the values and beliefs you have that made you behave that way. (Kim Fox)

Developing your identity as a reflective professional practitioner is also about recognising the change in personal understanding and practice.

> I initially considered reflection to only mean what something looked like, however I now understand that it can answer so many more questions including why, how and the impact of my actions on others. (Angela Dyer)

The reflective practitioner is in this sense represented as 'an intellectually curious person who rejects a passive approach to knowledge and prefers to construct knowledge together with others rather than simply "consume" it' (Rinaldi, 2005: 135). This would suggest that it is possible to learn and yet not fully open yourself up to the possibility of personal change. For example, avoiding critical examination of what you are 'choosing' to learn may result in easily assimilated 'knowledge' that does not challenge current assumptions or encourage independent interpretation. As the following examples from academic essays illustrate, the process of understanding yourself through reflective learning enables you to evaluate your thinking, understand the difference between deep rather than surface learning and to identify what has changed and what needs to change.

> My early understanding of the reflective process reflected 'single loop' rather than 'double loop' learning (Argyris and Schön, 1978). Single-loop learning seems to be present when goals, value frameworks and strategies are taken for granted (Smith, 2001). The emphasis is on changing the activity rather than the governing principles. I have since realised that reflection is a much deeper process. Bolton (2005) believes reflective practice can be risky and disruptive as it challenges us to look at our assumptions and prejudices and what we are avoiding, laying everything open to question. When these underlying norms, policies, values and principles are examined and questioned double-loop learning occurs. My main area of learning in this cycle was not in the initial issue but in my own attitude. (Sue Foster)

> Through further reading I was able to gain crucial knowledge about reflective intelligence also known as meta-learning or meta-cognition (Askew and Carnell, 1998) which includes strategies for self-monitoring, mental management and helping individuals create a positive attitude towards investing mental effort into issues. This helped me to understand that in order to move forward I needed to change my attitude. (Permjit Tanda)

These examples demonstrate the application of reflective thinking processes supported by the students' willingness to research different perspectives and to use these to self-evaluate and to inform personal change. However, identifying what is significant for you and internalising the evidence can be a challenge when the 'working memory' is overwhelmed by information from experience and other sources (Feuerstein, cited in Petty, 2004). If you are engaged in a programme of study, assessment of learning can also be an inhibiting factor as you struggle to construct personal meanings within someone else's framework and expectations. The act of constructing your personal meanings and developing your 'voice' or interpretation is, however, essential to the development of your identity, competence and confidence as a reflective professional practitioner.

Learning experiences

Learning experiences that have the potential to transform your way of thinking, to provide the cognitive challenge needed to stimulate the accommodation of different perspectives, can be an emotional as well as an intellectual experience.

> Initially, thinking about thoughts and actions – why I did something – why then – why that way – was it right – was it fair or good? Could I have done it better – should I have done it all? What encouraged me to do something or react that way? How can I improve? At a deeper level opening up to being vulnerable to risk. (Sue Foster)

> It's been really hard to make reflective practice become part of what I do. Reading about the theory of it only gives you so much – you have to do it to understand why it is so important. It's only when you do it that you can really get to grips with it. Even then it's still not easy and takes practice to get deep, not just superficially look at your practice. (Kim Fox)

How you respond to learning experiences can depend on your understanding of your role as learner and practitioner. For some, the belief that there is one 'right' answer limits the search for new ways of thinking, the use of the evidence and consequently the potential for new understandings and changes to the values and beliefs that inform their practice. In the following example Sammy-Jo has discovered the potential of reflective learning as a process that she now 'owns'.

> Since being in practice I have realised that I'm constantly thinking about the way we work with children, the theories behind our actions. I find myself reflecting in and on action more, I can question theorists and fellow practitioners' views and practice as well as my own. Being reflective means being open-minded about everything. There is no right or wrong answer ... I am now more confident in my ability to reflect as my understanding is that reflection is personal, never concrete, it is forever changing and challenging, a skill that takes a lifetime to perfect, if it can be perfected at all. Reflection is a skill which needs time, motivation and determination to be able to develop yourself ... It involves being strong enough to step beyond your 'comfort zone', challenge yourself and delve deeper into the situation – explore without an outcome in mind. (Sammy-Jo Morgan)

For Sammy-Jo, this ability to reflect involves more than learning a systematic approach or set of rules; she now feels confident that whilst recognising what others have to say about reflective practice she can and should make sense of it herself in terms of her own experience. She is also recognising that this is an ongoing process and, as Bolton (2005) suggests, is able to 'let go' and explore new possibilities.

Expressing and representing thought, feelings and experiences

The expression and representation of thoughts, feelings and experiences provides reflective practitioners with the means through which current understandings and new possibilities can be explored. Telling or writing our stories is in Bolton's (2005) view a reflective mode of thinking.

> Having the opportunity to recall a critical incident which is of significance has facilitated my understanding of reflective practice. It has made it easier to understand the relevance of theory and has also given me the opportunity to explore my own value base. (Permjit Tanda)

For many of the students on the course writing a reflective journal has proved to be a valuable tool for recording thoughts and feelings and as a stimulus for a deeper learning and personal change.

> I do not normally write a diary but through using a journal I have been able to reflect on my professional and personal identity and consequently move forward. (Rachel Challacombe)

> Engaging in a personal learning log has helped me to begin to think critically about my experiences ... it shows progression in the trust I have developed in being reflective as a way of developing as an early years practitioner and in personal change. (Shanna Bradley)

Although expressing thoughts in this way suits some people, discovering the best way for you to express yourself is part of the process of developing your identity as a reflective practitioner. Through personal experience Rachel and Shanna discovered for themselves the benefits of exploring a different approach. Writing poetry, creating diagrams or mind-maps are other approaches which have been used within a journal or as a separate process to support reflective thinking; the essential factor is finding methods which support your reflective thinking and learning process.

Reflective 'communities of learning and practice'

When considering the identification and development of an individual's identity as a reflective practitioner it is useful to consider Wenger's (1998: 4) view that 'learning as social participation shapes not only what we do, but also who we are and how we interpret what we do'. From this perspective, the reflective practitioner you are now, and the one you will become, has and will be influenced by the communities in which you learn and practice. The nature of the individuals within these communities and your interaction with them is likely to inform not only your reflective practice but also your identity and self-concept as a reflective practitioner. Sarah has discovered the benefits of this shared participation for reflective practice.

> Reflection involves taking a step back and trying to look at things from a different perspective ... it is something personal but sometimes it takes someone else to help you to discuss things, think them through and see it differently. (Sarah Rowberry)

Not only may you see things 'differently', you may also see yourself differently. Participating in a range of communities of learning and practice that offer different perspectives can help us to question and think more clearly about our values, actions and experiences. 'Communities of practice' in this sense is more a series of dynamic and fluid processes between different individuals in different contexts rather than a fixed term to describe a specific group or team. Depending on the nature of the issues being considered and the ethical issues involved, there is potential for colleagues, children and their families to be involved in a dynamic and stimulating reflective process, co-constructing knowledge, making and sharing meaning. Programmes of study that value and encourage 'shared participation' in the reflective learning process provide opportunities for students to work as a learning community.

> We were encouraged to discuss issues through online discussion, through face-to-face group participation and were presented with material which on occasions questioned our value base. Online discussions encouraged us within the safety of our groups to discuss issues and encouraged us to think laterally as described by De Bono (1990), the concept of exploring ideas with no solution in mind. We were learning the value of divergent and convergent thinking, the ability to generate alternative perspectives on problems rather than following standardised formats for problem solving. More importantly a safe environment had been created as recognised by Rogers (1967) in order for creative thinking to flow, which was especially important to my learning. (Permjit Tanda)

Within her writing Permjit is expressing and representing what she has learned about reflective practice as a creative process as well as her reflections on how she was learning; this in itself is an essential part of her learning process. Conferencing, whether online or face to face is one of many ways of creating a learning environment in which participants feel able and 'safe' to express their thoughts and share experiences without fear of being judged; it is possible to 'play' with ideas, explore possibilities, think critically about evidence and to 'create' new understandings through dialogue with others. However, although approaches such as conferencing can provide a valuable scaffold for dissemination, discussion and debate, the benefits are dependent on the willingness of the individuals involved to participate in the process and to recognise and value different professional identities (Anning et al., 2006). Involvement can be enhanced if the participants understand the role of learning and practice communities and how they can support their professional development.

Understanding how the communities you experience can and do work in practice and your role within them is part of the process of 'becoming a reflective practitioner', of understanding your professional identity. For example, if as Lieberman (2007: 199) states, 'learning communities become arenas for professional learning because the people imbue activities with shared meanings, develop a sense of belonging, and create new identities based, in part, on their relationships with one another', then each of us can have a role in nurturing positive relationships, in developing a 'safe environment' and a genuine sense of community in order to effect change. This is not always easy. Engestrom (1999, cited in Anning et al., 2006) argues that individuals with different knowledge and histories need a shared vision for the future whilst 'articulating differences, exploring alternatives, modelling solutions, examining an agreed model and implementing activities' (Anning et al., 2006: 11). Practitioners who can lead the development of a reflective community of practice are likely to be experienced in the reflective process, confident in their own personal perspective, professional identity and role as a learner and member of the community. Consequently, they are able to recognise and value different strengths and approaches while acknowledging that everyone's journey is different.

The wider context

Campbell et al. (2004: 10) argue that the 'reflective practitioner is by definition a researcher, researching not just their own professional context but, crucially, researching that context as they act within it'. Bolton (2005: 5) however, reminds us that reflective practice should go beyond personal 'navel-gazing' and be examined in terms of wider social and political structures. Extending our participation in communities of learning and practice beyond everyday experience is essential for the development of personal and shared understandings and re-evaluation of values and practices. A commitment to personal change as evidence-based practitioners (Campbell et al., 2004) or practitioner researchers (Campbell et al., 2004), through reading and participation in events such as conferences, special interest groups and professional bodies, will facilitate the ongoing process of examining and challenging issues from different perspectives.

> Reading recommended texts on reflective practice has stimulated me to think more deeply about me and my thoughts. I challenge my own beliefs and after consideration and evaluation facilitate change in my practice both in and out of the childcare setting. (Lianne Piggott)

This process of continuing professional development can also include your role in disseminating your own research and the insights gained to a wider audience. The pictures of practice examined within this book provide insights into other ways of being, experiencing, perceiving and practising. What is important is the way we as individuals and as communities of practice process the evidence; that we adopt a critical stance supported by existing knowledge and understandings. In this way reflective practice becomes a tool not only for enlightenment but also a tool for empowerment. Theory provides us with a range of tools that can help us with the process of 'meta-reflection', to help us understand our professional identity as reflective practitioners, to support the processes in practice and to evaluate the outcomes. We can apply theoretical frameworks and models to help us recognise what is significant and to give us the confidence to apply some of the principles and insights in ways we might not have previously. It is essential that we utilise good quality tools and materials, but it is the way that these are used that enables the practitioner to think critically and creatively and to develop beyond the role of the worker-as-technician (Moss, 2008: xiii).

Summary

How can we as reflective practitioners aspire to be effective 'change agents' within our professional roles and contribute to the process of ensuring positive outcomes for children if we do not understand who we are, what we are about, why we do what we do and how this is being achieved? How can we support others within our 'communities of practice' if we do not understand our own learning journey and understand

(Continued)

(Continued)

and value the journeys experienced by others? This chapter has examined why it is essential that as individuals and professionals, whether front-line practitioners, managers, policy makers or lecturers, we articulate and have confidence in our developing identity as reflective practitioners and what this involves. We should take ownership of the reflective process as individuals and within communities of learning and practice, supported by a commitment to personal change and to learning from and with others within and beyond our personal experience. The chapters that follow will provide you with an opportunity to extend the range of your learning experience, to explore different insights, theories and practice. Whilst reading them, 'listen' to the voices of reflection, explore what they are saying about their identity and the implications for their practice. Reflect on how this relates to you and your learning journey.

Postscript

Email from a colleague:

Hi Karen, read your chapter ... but have you thought about the impact of Wenger's communities of practice?

Extract from reflective diary:

Oh no, I thought I had finished ... here I go again ... but do I want to think about this again? ... It is a good point though ... If I just do a little more reading we can talk about it tomorrow ...

Suggested further reading

- Bolton, G. (2005) *Reflective Practice: Writing and Professional Development.* 2nd edn. London: Sage Publications.
  This book discusses the importance of reflective practice for professional development. It analyses how reflective practice can support both personal and interdisciplinary knowledge and understanding.

- Paige-Smith, A. and Craft, A. (eds) (2007) *Developing Reflective Practice in the Early Years*. Buckingham: Open University Press.
  This book provides a comprehensive view of professional practice. It underlines the importance of reflection on practice to improve professional development.

References

Anning, A., Cottrell, D., Frost, N., Green, J. and Robinson, M. (2006) *Developing Multiprofessional Teamwork for Integrated Children's Services*. London: McGraw-Hill.

Argyris, C. and Schön, D. (1978) *Organisational Learning*. Reading, MA: Addison Wesley.

Askew, S. and Carnell, E. (1998) *Transforming Learning: Individual and Global Change*. London: Cassell.

Bertram, T. and Owen, S. (2007) 'Raise your game'. http://www.nurseryworld.co.uk/news/722622/Raise-game/ (accessed 16.01.2009).

Bolton, G. (2005) *Reflective Practice: Writing and Professional Development*. 2nd edn. London: Sage Publications.

Brookfield, S. (1995) *Becoming a Critically Reflective Teacher*. San Francisco, CA: Jossey-Bass.

Campbell, A., McNamara, O. and Gilroy, P. (2004) *Practitioner Research and Professional Development in Education*. London: Paul Chapman Publishing.

Claxton, G. (2003) *The Intuitive Practitioner: On the Value of Not Always Knowing What One Is Doing*. Maidenhead: Open University Press.

Children's Workforce Development Council (CWDC) (2008) *Guidance to the Standards for the Award of the Early Years Professional Status*. Leeds: CWDC Publications.

Clough, P. and Corbett, J. (2000) *Theories of Inclusive Education*. London: Paul Chapman Publishing.

De Bono, E. (1990) *Lateral Thinking*. London: Penguin Books.

Department for Children, Schools and Families (DCSF) (2008) *The Early Years Foundation Stage*. Nottingham: DCSF Publications.

Department for Education and Skills (DfES) (2005) *Common Core of Skills and Knowledge for the Children's Workforce*. Nottingham: DfES.

Lieberman, A. (2007) 'Professional learning communities', in L. Stoll and L.K. Seashore (eds), *Professional Learning Communities: Divergence, Depth and Dilemmas*. Maidenhead: Open University Press.

Moon, J. (2008) *Critical Thinking: An Exploration of Theory and Practice*. London: Routledge.

Moss, P. (2008) 'Foreword', in A. Paige-Smith and A. Craft, *Developing Reflective Practice in the Early Years*. Maidenhead: Open University Press.

Penney, W. and Warelow, P. (1999) 'Understanding the prattle of praxis', *Nursing Inquiry*, 6(4): 259–68.

Petty, G. (2004) *Teaching Today*. 3rd edn. Cheltenham: Nelson Thornes.

Rinaldi, C. (2005) *In Dialogue with Reggio Emilia: Listening, Researching and Learning*. London: Routledge.

Rogers, C. (1967) *A Therapist's View of Psychotherapy on Becoming a Person*. London: Constable.

Schön, D. (1983) *The Reflective Practitioner: How Professionals Think in Action*. New York: Basic Books.

Schön, D. (1987) *Educating the Professional Practitioner*. San Francisco, CA: Jossey-Bass.

Smith, M. (2001) 'Donald Schon: learning, reflection and change'. http://www.infed.org/thinkers/et-schon.htm (accessed 25.08.2008).

Wenger, E. (1998) *Communities of Practice: Learning, Meaning and Identity*. Cambridge: Cambridge University Press.

2

Play in the Early Years Foundation Stage

Natalie Canning

Chapter objectives

This chapter reflects on the benefits of play for the developing child. It argues that play provides a foundation for the well-being of children which encompasses health, physical growth and strength, emotional development, problem solving and social interaction (DCMS, 2006). It suggests that play provides a platform for children to learn about risks and use their own initiative. Play involves practising skills and consolidating friendships, learning how to negotiate with others and contributing to the way children emerge as emotionally aware and sensitive individuals. Play and learning is at the heart of many early years settings; and this chapter considers the relationship in practice between the rhetoric of the Early Years Foundation Stage (EYFS) guidance and the reality of locating play at the centre of early childhood learning experiences. Throughout, a central theme of the chapter is an examination of the challenges for practitioners when providing play-based practice and the following themes are also explored:

- perspectives of play within early years practice which consider play as a process with opportunities to learn or play as a vehicle for structured activities to meet required outcomes;

(Continued)

(Continued)

- the interconnectedness of play and learning and the importance of the environment and the role of the practitioner, in providing quality experiences for children;
- reflections from practitioners regarding the importance of play within the practice guidance for the EYFS and the implementation of this in practice.

Kalliala provides a view of play that suggests: 'Play paves the way for later development and learning. Children seem to learn various skills while playing and generate "learning products" ... Children don't play in order to learn although they do learn through play' (2006: 20).

This implies that children's involvement in play starts from what they are already able to do and what they feel comfortable with. Initially children enter into play with a certain amount of knowledge about the situation, for example:

- who is already involved in the play;
- whether the play is something that they are interested in;
- the materials that are involved in the play at the point of showing interest;
- where the play is taking place.

This knowledge locates children in a position of confidence where they have actively chosen to be part of the play situation. Play may change, become more challenging or be directed by other children, but the child makes a decision based on the information they have, how much they want to be involved and how confident they feel in being accepted into the play situation. Rieber (1996) suggests that when children volunteer in active engagement with others, it liberates their creative and imaginative thinking which supports quality interactions and learning opportunities. It promotes children's ability to enter into a journey of discovery with other children through creating a play situation which is meaningful, exciting and sustains their interest. It also enables their ability to explore the environment of their play. The intrinsic worth that play provides for children supports opportunities for optimal life experiences (Kalliala, 2006). This view underlines the point that sensations children experience in their play are revisited, for example, children re-enter the same play situation over a period of time or take a particular scenario into another form of play. They might include the same children or others in the play they are revisiting and play in the same environment or extend it into new experiences. The ability for children to revisit same play experiences liberates children to support and control their own play development. Critically, the emotional value of play is remembered by the child, perhaps not consciously in that moment, but every play experience contains a link to future holistic development, that is, how a child learns as well as what they learn. This does not mean that play is always an easy experience, but the challenge and difficulty children bring to play is motivated from their desire to achieve their own goals (Sutton Smith, 1997). The way in which play is constructed between children means that they are able to connect with the situation and others involved in the play to make sense and meaning, problem solve and learn from each other.

Point for reflection

- Can you recognise the difference between providing play opportunities and planning activities to promote play?
- In your practice how much of your time is spent providing opportunities for play?
- How much of your time is spent planning and organising activities to promote play?

If you spend time considering how to plan for the process of play, rich opportunities for observation and assessment of children's learning are created.

Implications for practice – play as an act or object?

One aspect of play that researchers agree upon is that the term 'play' is difficult to define (Anning and Edwards, 2006; Fisher, 2008; Hughes, 2006; Kalliala, 2006; Moyles, 2005). Play involves so many developmental characteristics that theories of play provide different perspectives on the element which is significant to them, whether that be cognitive development (Piaget, 1962), emotional well-being (MacMahon, 1992), learning (Vygotsky, 1978) or socialisation (Bandura, 1962), to name a few.

Dau (1999) suggests that defining play depends on how play is seen:

- as an object: what is play?
- or as an act: what happens in play in terms of creating meaning?

Arguably, both perspectives are important and intertwined. To understand the way in which children engage in play, the rich material that is created from play, and the subsequent opportunities offered to children to revisit and build on existing experiences cannot be developed without an understanding of the meaning of play.

Dau suggests that even though the 'object of play' and the 'act of play' may be interlinked and dependent upon each other, there is a clear divide in how they are approached. The act of play recognises the child at the centre of the play process, whilst the object of play is concerned with a quantifiable outcome from play engagement. The differing approaches are important in considering the way in which play opportunities are offered within a setting and also in thinking about how the EYFS is constructed. If the *act* of play is nurtured, then the *object* of play naturally emerges. However, if the object of play is the central concern then the act of play becomes lost in striving for the ultimate outcome. One is located from a child-centred perspective of emergent play, based on discovering interests and building learning opportunities from the child's lead, whilst the other plans the activities of the day or week based on the outcomes identified as needing to be met. Practitioners' experiences of observing and recording play opportunities is demonstrated through a reflective process where the act of play is paramount and therefore the object of play can be defined.

Point for reflection

- Why is it important to have a detailed understanding of the way in which play is an important facet of each child's individual development?
- Play provides a way in which you can observe and understand how children learn as well as what they are learning. How do you facilitate this in your setting?

EYFS guidance on play: rhetoric and reality

The Early Years Foundation Stage (EYFS) recognises play as underpinning practice. It states:

> Play underpins all development and learning for young children. Most children play spontaneously, although some may need adult support and it is through play that they develop intellectually, creatively, physically, socially and emotionally. (DCSF, 2008: 7)

It also stresses the importance of the practitioner's role to support children in making sense of the world, developing their skills, concepts and ideas. The EYFS suggests that this is done through 'planning to make learning effective, exciting, varied and progressive' (DCSF, 2008: 12). Practitioners are encouraged to observe and reflect on spontaneous play and then plan and resource a challenging environment to support and extend areas of learning. Fisher (2008) acknowledges that spontaneous play provides the richest source of observational evidence for practitioners, but also recognises that spontaneity cannot be predicted by the adult. In adult-free play, children determine their own rules, the direction of their play and the level of involvement they participate in. From a retrospective point of view, planning to develop interests of the child which emerge from spontaneous play may be possible. However, the nature of spontaneity means that children will also combine their play with other interests to develop and trigger other forms of imagination and creativity.

Point for reflection

- Do you consider creativity an important facet of play?
- If this is the case, how do we encourage creativity as part of spontaneous actions that the child makes in relation to their own learning, relationships with others and the adults who care for them?

Play in practice

Practitioners from private day nurseries, pre-schools and childminders in the South West of England were asked to give their experiences of play and learning in practice. They were asked to quantify any effect the introduction of the EYFS has had on practice and whether they consider their setting to be process driven or outcome led.

A picture of practice – childminder setting

A childminder reflected on a recent play interaction with a 3½-year-old boy. He was completely immersed in playing with some kitchen foil. He ripped it up into small pieces and was making it into different shapes. He asked, 'Which do you like best?' and proceeded to inform her that they were 'transformers'. He demonstrated this by taking one of the foil shapes and squeezing it in his hand to change it into another shape – 'see', he said, 'it's transformed!' This insight into the child's play demonstrates the spontaneity of his interest and how he developed the play further by transforming the foil. The play was motivated and sustained by the child for approximately 20 minutes. During the day the child continued to return to the transformer play and consequently the childminder was left with foil deposits all around her house!

This experience could potentially be revisited depending on the 'act' or process of play that the child decided upon. The children in the setting have a high level of autonomy in their play because it is completely child-centred. The childminder reflected that she would not change this because of the EYFS but felt pressured to record more articulate observations. She suggested that providing 'proof' that the EYFS is being followed has created more paperwork. In the setting, free play opportunities emerge naturally and the childminder reflected that it was impossible to plan for the spontaneity that comes from the children and herself, for example if it is a nice day they may decide to go to the beach or up to the moors. Such flexibility in childminding ensures that there are opportunities to meet individual needs. In implementing the EYFS this has not changed her practice, but has added to the complexity of recording it. To overcome this, a structured activity is planned once a month to produce written evidence that children are achieving outcomes outlined in the EYFS and these are recorded under the six areas of learning:

1. personal, social and emotional development;
2. communication, language and literacy;
3. problem solving, reasoning and numeracy;
4. knowledge and understanding of the world;
5. physical development;
6. creative development

In developing observations which record more information under the four principles she uses a daily diary. Through this process she acknowledges she has become more focused on the 'object' of play in these activities. She reflected that initially the documentation was threatening and she felt that it was a way in which practitioners were being asked to conform. Interestingly, she is undertaking a Foundation Degree in Early Years and explained that through developing her knowledge on the course she would now feel more confident and able to justify her approach to play, learning and development.

The practitioners' role in play

One of the challenges of defining play is that it is part of a child's construct where frequently adults are excluded as children enter their own world of discovery. Children have their own agenda of play which is flexible depending on the environment, resources available and children involved. Samuelsson and Johansson (2006) regard play as children's 'life-world', where children experience their surrounding environment intertwined with learning opportunities in which they live–social, cultural and historical influences. Play is a process from which learning evolves to support children's development. They view 'lived experiences as the key to influencing children's understanding and actions in the surrounding world' (Samuelsson and Johansson, 2006: 50)

In considering play as a process the inherent value of play is central to the development of children. Hughes (2001) states play is intrinsically motivated from within children and that they need to play to sustain their ability to engage with the physical and emotional world. From this perspective play becomes more than an object or platform for developing skills but an indicator for the personality of the child. When children engage in play they reflect the day-to-day aspects of their lives and model the behaviour of those that are significant to them. They are engaged in the development of their feelings, attitudes and belief systems alongside their practical and physical skills. Hughes categorises this as 'deep play' as it constitutes children's 'immediate reality and provides a reflection of the level of children's connection with their immediate environment' (2006: 23).

The challenge for practitioners is that a process-driven concept of play requires a holistic and long-term approach in developing strategies for recording and monitoring learning and development. In early years settings play is usually explored by practitioners in 'mini episodes' where play is depicted in the context of the moment, examining the actions, connections and emotions that emerge from play that is sustained for a period of time. The focus is on particular children or situations which prescribe to a definition of play or object approach adopted by the setting. Within this context practitioners demonstrate their ability to observe children and record their skills and learning in a 'snapshot' of time. In managing play in this way children are given the opportunity for relatively short play episodes in a justifiable and outcome-led system. As settings become caught in a cycle of accountability and justification towards children's learning and development, 'play' has become part of the tick sheet mentality towards early childhood. A practitioner reflected:

> For the requirements of the assessment in the EYFS our setting is attempting to do learning journeys for each child. What we have found is that we spend so much time doing these – trying not to make them just a tick list – that we don't spend the quality time with the children. (Pre-school Manager, July 2008)

The EYFS suggests that 'flexible plans are required by the setting to adapt to circumstances' (DCSF, 2008: 12) and that the observations that practitioners collect link children's play to where they are in terms of learning. In turn this should provide ideas of how to support extensions of learning in the future. One practitioner commented: 'this sounds good on paper, but in reality is more difficult to achieve'. Practitioners have to develop skills not just in observing and recording the object or outcomes of play, but also recording the act of play and processes each individual child contributes to how the play is developed. For practical reasons, this leads to an approach of logical thinking and planning which ultimately results in adult-directed delivery of play. Fisher (2008) identifies three approaches to play:

- adult-focused on small group work with children;
- adult-initiated arising from planning;
- child-initiated experiences created by the child.

Fisher suggests that these approaches should be equally balanced by the setting to provide appropriate learning experience for children. However, in practice the adult-led and adult-focused activities tend to dominate sessions as they are planned by the practitioner to a clear aim and outcome. This restricts children's freedom of choice and creativity, but is arguably easy to observe and record to meet the six areas of learning.

> In [the setting] we would like to engage in more free play opportunities for children, but in reality I don't know how we can provide a curriculum based on what we perceive as play. The adult led and initiated activities take over because we can then clearly record the requirements for the EYFS. (Lead Practitioner, private day nursery, July 2008)

To observe children in play that has naturally derived from their own ideas and motivation is a skill which requires a holistic mentality of early childhood and approach to learning. Katz (1998) refers to children as not targets of instruction, but having the role of an active apprentice where they work alongside others in the discovery of solutions to questions and problems that are meaningful to them. The play that emerges from this approach may not on the surface look any different from an adult-initiated activity, yet the philosophy and the process of how children reach that point is considerably different. Children emerge as their own directors of play and learning. It is then the practitioner's role to reflect on how children reached that point and the level of involvement needed from them to support the play. In practice, planning which attempts to reflect flexibility in following and predicting child-initiated play often results in very loose sweeping statements which ultimately are not used and provide only lip-service to meet the expectations of the documentation being followed.

A picture of practice – private day nursery setting

A practitioner recounted a play situation where children had enjoyed an adult-led play session with toy farm animals. The children had been counting the different types of animals and putting the pigs in the pig pen, horses in their stable, cows in the field, and so on. One child made links with his play and Noah's Ark at which point the practitioner followed the child's lead and brought a toy ark into the play space and the children continued to count the animals into the ark. The practitioner responded to the spontaneity of the children's ideas and links made with previous learning by fetching the toy ark and placing it next to the animal characters. She was sensitive to the change in direction of the play and supported the connections the children had made between current play, past play and family experiences, knowledge and understanding.

One child articulated that it was difficult for the animals to get into the ark and that what they really needed was a bridge. Later in the day the children accessed the building blocks and junk material to build a bridge for the animals to more easily enter the ark. The flexibility in the play and setting environment afforded children the opportunity to engage in free play with no adult direction or input.

The setting provided flexibility for the children to be spontaneous within a planned play activity. They were then able to have the confidence and curiosity to revisit the play and extend the content and context to support their own interests. Equally the practitioner was not aware that the children would make such play connections and therefore could not have pre-planned the scenario for the extension of the activity. The practitioner reflected that the

(Continued)

(Continued)

children were able to support their own interests through play because the setting did not place any restrictions on play materials and enabled children to discover their own interests by providing a high proportion of adult-free play time with open and flexible approaches to play directed from the child's interests.

Moss and Petrie (2002) refer to 'children's spaces' as providing possibilities for play and learning which are child initiated without predetermined outcomes. They acknowledge that for true children's spaces to occur the practitioner needs to risk that they will not know what the outcome of the play may be or that they will not be in complete control. This creates a tension as although many practitioners would agree that play should occur in spaces which empower children to make choices and direct their own play experiences, they feel restricted by the perceived outcome-led directives that the EYFS imposes.

The importance of play

Practitioners value the use of children's spaces for their own experiences and motivation to discover, socialise, problem solve and communicate, and agree that this is the most powerful and meaningful learning experience. A paradox exists between wanting to allow children to play and develop from their intrinsic motivation to do so and an adult culture which is driven by achievement, outcome and progression. This is evident by the following statement in the EYFS:

> You must undertake the EYFS Profile for all children of an appropriate age and assess them through observational assessment against the 13 scales and report 13 scores for each child. (DCSF, 2008: 13)

The reality for the majority of practitioners is that the EYFS is less complicated to implement if they arrange adult-focused and initiated activities around the six areas of learning. This enables evidence to be clearly linked to the 13 scales and scores. Pockets of child-initiated play may then be slotted into the routine of the setting to acknowledge the importance of adult-free play. This routine satisfies the outcome-led culture which early childhood seems to have unquestionably accepted as the norm. It reflects on play as an object within a process rather than the beginning, middle and end of children's experiences. The rhetoric is that play is a central aspect of the EYFS, yet the ability to position it at the heart of every child's learning experience is overshadowed by infrastructure of targets and standards.

Consequently, in the adult world, play has developed a reputation for being fun or doing something that comes after something more important. Rieber (1996: 43) identifies that there is a misconception that 'play is easy and is therefore more appropriate after a "serious" or structured learning activity'. When play is represented in these terms it demands little respect from the adult world. Samuelsson and Johansson (2006) identify that through a play process children are also productive, but the difference is that children form the goals from within their play. This is supported through the Reggio Emilia philosophy towards learning where children are 'authors of their own learning' (Malaguzzi, 1994: 55). Children in negotiation with practitioners and one another determine the course of their play, investigation and learning (Hewett, 2001). This approach to play and learning development demonstrates how both the act and object of play can coexist and complement each other. However, to enable the interplay between the perspectives of act and object the culture of the setting needs to adopt the same philosophy and needs to be supported by a structure which fosters a process-driven play curriculum over outcome-led targets.

The interconnectedness of play

Using the vehicle of play, children become skilled at being open to new experiences and using those new experiences to meet their own curiosity, creativity and exploration needs. Play creates independent thinkers where opportunities for participation and action support children's development and learning (Anning and Edwards, 2006). Play opportunities which are meaningful to children provide rich learning environments to support children's development. The interconnectedness of play and learning means that in any play situation, a learning opportunity is also evident. This is not always obvious to the child engaged in the play, yet the learning is implicit within the social connections the child engages with and the new skills and attributes which emerge.

Samuelsson and Johansson (2006) discuss the difficulties that the interconnectedness of play and learning has presented in Swedish pre-schools. The perspective of play adopted in the past has been to support children in constructing and maintaining their play without disturbing them.

> Children's play has not been included in the learning process ... [it] should be protected and kept free, joyful and carefree. (Samuelsson and Johansson, 2006: 48)

Play and learning have been seen as separate identities, each being valued, but emerging from different processes, school-based activities and freedom of children to play. As Sweden moved towards the integration of play and learning within their pre-school curriculum Samuelsson and Johansson (2006) identify that the ability of teachers to unfold and integrate dimensions of learning in play and play in learning is a skill in itself. Practitioners in England face the same dilemma, as using play to demonstrate children's intellectual and social growth is a process which requires investment in time and developing a philosophy within the setting so that every aspect of practice supports the process. The long-term results are not easily quantifiable in the short term and, without a learning culture which supports a process-driven identity, this places practitioners in a position where they feel they need to defend their approach.

The EYFS supports a move towards observation, assessment and planning around the six areas of learning. It argues a practitioner-led principled approach to working with children. For practitioners who are already effective in providing a stimulating learning environment the EYFS argues that their practice will not need to change (DCSF, 2008). However, it is clear that some practitioners felt they were being asked to constantly 'prove' their professional capabilities and justify how their beliefs with regard to the interconnectedness of play and learning could work within their setting, especially if the setting provided free-flow play opportunities. One practitioner commented: 'How can you plan to be spontaneous in play?'.

These views should be seen alongside a realisation that the environment is central to process-driven play and learning experiences for children. An environment which is flexible in terms of offering children the opportunity for self-directed play, creativity and exploration encourages independent thinking for children to develop as self-motivated learners. In providing such an environment, practitioners need knowledge and understanding of the influence of their surroundings. Broadhead (2006) recognises that practitioners need to begin from an informed understanding of learning which is often developed from observing children in their play environments. Consequently, the assumptions that practitioners hold regarding an appropriate environment to stimulate children's learning shapes the early childhood experiences they are exposed to (David, 2003). The EYFS stresses the importance of the practitioner in the involvement of children's play and development (DCSF, 2008: 7), however, this requires the practitioner to have substantial knowledge of how play progresses in early childhood and how learning can be supported through play.

Summary

There is a need to enter into a continuous dialogue between practitioners to explore preconceptions and expectations individuals may have of children. In order to reflect on practice there should be open communication, not just between practitioners, but also with families and across different types of settings. This dialogue supports knowledge and understanding and is especially important with regards to the way in which practitioners interpret play and the value they place on it. The EYFS places emphasis on learning outcomes for the child. For these to come to fruition, values and perspectives of play amongst practitioners need to be clear and practice needs to reflect these. This will provide the setting with a belief system on how to provide children with the opportunities to learn through a process of play. Across the country, workshops have been held for practitioners on the implementation of the EYFS. A key question to ask is: have these focused on paperwork, observation, planning and assessment or have they addressed play-based practice? Are they considering the 'object' or 'act' of play? Care is needed, to ensure that we do not place too much emphasis on valuing what we are able to measure rather than measuring what we truly value.

Suggested further reading

- Hughes, B. (2001) *Evolutionary Playwork and Reflective Analytical Practice.* London: Routledge.

  Hughes argues in this book that play is a crucial component in the development of all children and explores the complexities of children's play, its meaning and purpose.

- Kalliala, M. (2006) *Play Culture in a Changing World.* Buckingham: Open University Press.

  Kalliala considers how children's play reflects children's experiences and evaluates the importance of play in childhood.

References

Anning, A. and Edwards, A. (2006) *Promoting Children's Learning from Birth to Five: Developing the New Early Years Professional.* 2nd edn. Maidenhead: Open University Press.

Bandura, A. (1962) 'Social learning through imitation', in M.R. Jones (ed.), *Nebraska Symposium on Motivation.* Chicago, IL: University of Chicago Press.
Broadhead, P. (2006) 'Developing an understanding of young children's learning through play: the place of observation, interaction and reflection', *British Educational Research Journal,* 32(2): 191–207.
Dau, E. (1999) *Child's Play: Revisiting Play in Early Childhood Settings.* Sydney: Maclennan and Petty.
David, T. (2003) *What Do We Know about Teaching Young Children?* London: British Education Research Association Early Years Special Interest Group.
Department for Children, Schools and Families (DCSF) (2008) *Practice Guidance for the Early Years Foundation Stage.* Nottingham: DCSF.
Department for Culture, Media and Sport (DCMS) (2006) *Time for Play: Encouraging Greater Play Opportunities for Children and Young People.* London: Department for Culture, Media and Sport.
Fisher, J. (2008) *Starting from the Child.* 3rd edn. Buckingham: Open University Press/McGraw-Hill.
Hewett, V. (2001) 'Examining the Reggio Emilia approach to early childhood education', *Early Childhood Education Journal,* 29(2): 95–100.
Hughes, B. (2001) *Evolutionary Playwork and Reflective Analytical Practice.* London: Routledge.
Hughes, B. (2006) *Play Types: Speculations and Possibilities.* London: Centre for Playwork Education and Training.
Kalliala, M. (2006) *Play Culture in a Changing World.* Buckingham: Open University Press.
Katz, L. (1998) 'What can we learn from Reggio Emilia?', in C. Edwards, L. Gandini and G. Forman (eds), *The Hundred Languages of Children: The Reggio Emilia Approach to Early Childhood Education.* 2nd edn. London: JAI Press.
MacMahon, L. (1992) *The Handbook of Play Therapy.* London: Routledge.
Malaguzzi, L. (1994) 'Your image of the child: where teaching begins', *Childcare Information Exchange,* (3): 52–61.
Moss, P. and Petrie, P. (2002) *From Children's Services to Children's Spaces.* London: Routledge.
Moyles, J. (2005) 'Introduction', in J. Moyles (ed.), *The Excellence of Play.* 2nd edn. Maidenhead: Open University Press.
Piaget, J. (1962) *Play Dreams and Imitation in Childhood.* London: Routledge and Kegan Paul.
Rieber, L. (1996) 'Seriously considering play: designing interactive learning environments based on the blending of microworlds, simulations and games', *Education Technology Research and Development Journal,* 44(2): 43–58.
Samuelsson, I. and Johansson, E. (2006) 'Play and learning – inseparable dimensions in pre-school practice', *Early Child Development and Care,* 176(1): 47–65.
Sutton Smith, B. (1997) *The Ambiguity of Play.* London: Harvard University Press.
Vygotsky, L. (1978) *Mind and Society.* Cambridge, MA: Harvard University Press.

3

21st Century Digital Technology and Children's Learning

Linda Tyler

Chapter objectives

This chapter considers technology used in early years settings or what we can call 'digital practice' with children. It attempts to answer some questions of interest to practitioners:

- Why is mastering technology important for children today and what may inhibit the development of 'digital practice in the early years'?
- Can technology underpin some commonly held views on the way children learn through play?
- Why is mastering technology important for children today?

NEWS FLASH! The world is changing! Without doubt, technology will continue to advance at speed so whether we like it or not children will need to develop skills for the 'techno age'. Indeed, technology already permeates all elements of our existence and is transforming our lives by making information and communication accessible. Over 85 per cent of households in the United Kingdom now have access to broadband, compared with only

8 per cent of households five years ago (BECTa, 2008: online). It is probable that more young children see their parents on a computer (mobile or static) or playing on a games console such as a Wii or Playstation than reading a book. Hsi (2006) acknowledges that many of today's teenagers have grown up in a world in which their preferred form of engagement and entertainment is mediated by technology. This technology has been part of a social revolution, which has made an increasingly digital world 'smaller'; a view not intended to advocate that we throw out the old to bring in the new, only to consider how current early childhood theory can be applied to the digital world we live in today and, moreover, to explore how technology can be integrated into the early years curriculum.

Donaldson's (1986) theory of children playing, learning and developing within a familiar context is a useful point to start. We need to examine what a familiar context means for children today and question whether we are supporting children in a context which is 'comfortable' for us rather than familiar to them. Prensky (2008) reminds us that life for children today may be a lot of things, but it is certainly not un-engaging; except in school. He is alerting us to the fact that children, when faced with nothing to do, will themselves 'find' something 'digital' to do to fill in their time. We need to make ourselves aware of children's home experiences with technology so that we build on what they know and can do. Information and communication technology (ICT) is not just about computers! Indeed, home-based computers are a very small part of the production of digital technology worldwide.

Used by educators or children digital cameras can be a means to track children's progress and inform future planning. Importantly they can give children a voice as evidenced by the work of Clark and Moss (2001) and play a significant part in listening to the voices of children. This can also be done using an 'ordinary' disposable camera shared between home and school. I was recently involved in a project where children (with their parents' consent) used cameras to photograph items they liked and disliked at home and in school. Talking through the pictures with them gave a superb insight into their interests, personalities, abilities and friendships, and allowed them to share and sustain their thinking. The Early Years Foundation Stage (EYFS) practice guidance declares that the most effective settings are those in which practitioners support and challenge children's thinking by getting involved in the thinking process with them (DCSF, 2008). The camera also facilitates stronger links between home and school. Indeed, there was enhanced dialogue between parents and children during the project.

Another project was called ICTogether. This allowed me to discreetly uncover a family's 'digital history'. I would spend one afternoon each week together with parents. I would support their understanding of how and why children used technology by getting them to interact with the technology themselves. This enabled them to develop their own skills and empowered them to better support their children at home. Children would also be involved and later join their parents, and each would share what they knew of that technology so that the knowledge became embedded. From this, I had an idea of what resources they had at home and what children and parents were able to do with them. Please note – this relied on old-fashioned personal, positive contact with parents, not becoming a modern day 'digital whiz kid'. It also underpinned the content of the EYFS, which argues that planning should be based around the children's interests and individual needs (DCSF, 2008).

Point for reflection

Technology, at its basic level, should allow for new and different ways of doing familiar tasks, and finding out about new resources. In the not-too-distant future some technologies will be as commonplace to today's children as mobile phones are to us. Of course, there is a need to be cautious and not try to run before we can walk. Nevertheless, am I starting to move you to consider a question posed at the outset – why is mastering technology important for children today?

An example from practice

Television and radio are always telling us that we can listen to a 'Podcast'. A Podcast is like a radio show but rather than being broadcast live, it is pre-recorded then distributed. In its simplest form a Podcast can be saved onto a memory stick/CD and shared with children or parents in this 'hard copy' way. I consider there are five key areas of Podcasting when working with younger children.

Explore/Play	Listen to other Podcasts! Put them into the book or quiet corner or role play area. Let the children discover what a Podcast is and enjoy it. A super site for young children is: www.storynory.com. WHY? Because children see and/or use Podcasting technology at home. They may have MP3 players, portable CD/Karaoke players which can also record, mobile phones, recording microphones or digital voice recorders. Practitioners should be providing these 'familiar' technologies in the setting.
Plan	Lots of thinking and questioning – there are many opportunities for literacy through speaking, listening, responding, group work and possibly drama. Children can share news, stories, songs, work, interviews, jokes, adverts, instructions – the list is endless. • Who will be the audience? • Will this change how we do things? Of course, all good radio shows need a jingle and as a Podcast mirrors a radio broadcast in many ways, exploring sounds and music is another exciting aspect of Podcasting.
Create	Start talking – make a Podcast! Because it is not broadcast as it is produced there is opportunity to evaluate and improve before it is broadcast. Children can listen to their own work and decide on improvements themselves.
Distribute	Publish the Podcast by putting it onto a CD or flash drive so it can be shared between classes or rooms or sent home to parents. Imagine the pleasure children will get from this – writing for a larger audience! Upload it to a website or setting network. What a super way to improve home/setting partnerships. Podcasts can be listened to by anyone at anytime. Wow! This simple process has opened up endless possibilities!
Advertise	We want an audience so how will we advertise? Will it stay in the setting or be shared with a wider audience including parents and extended family? Can we draw posters, hold a meeting, use word of mouth? Ask the children. Let them be involved with all the decisions.

Figure 3.1 Key areas of Podcasting and how they may look in practice

Figure 3.1 examines what each key area might look like in an early years setting.

If you are wondering how younger children can independently use a microphone to make a Podcast, look at Easi-Speak (Terrific Teaching

Solutions, 2008) which lets children record directly into the microphone and download files straight onto the computer through a USB connection. This can enhance literacy through speaking and listening, allowing children to add to what they do with paper and pencil.

Can technology underpin the way children are motivated to learn and learn through play?

Children born and raised in the 21st century require different pedagogical approaches. However these 'different pedagogical approaches' need careful consideration as the British Educational Communications and Technology Agency (BECTa) (DfES, 2003: 4) suggests: 'Teachers' pedagogies and pedagogical reasoning influence their uses of ICT and thereby pupils' attainment.' For example, a multi-sensory mix of auditory and visual digital cues encourages participation that is both engaging and motivating for young children. However, they can also deliver a new 'techno stress' by placing greater demands on a practitioner's own digital capabilities. A point that reveals a climate of mixed standpoints on the effectiveness of technology use in the classroom (Clements and Sarama, 2003; Cordes and Miller, 2000; Haugland, 1999; Wartella and Jennings, 2000). An easy way forward in the debate would of course be to argue that the 'proof is in the pudding' and there is no need to follow a digital pathway until there is strong evidence that the route leads to a recognised benefit for the children. However, an important part of a practitioner's job is to provide an environment which motivates and stimulates children as they explore it. Bergen (2004, cited in Saracho and Spodek, 2008) suggests that every object in an environment gives children 'affordances' that elicit actions. Affordances suggest ways objects can be used in work or play. Some objects will provide multiple affordances whilst others will be more limited. For example, construction kits offer children a multiplicity of how they can be played with (multiple affordances) but a jigsaw is designed with a specific affordance in mind. Bergen acknowledges a jigsaw has a short period of interest for a child whereas construction kits can sustain their interest for longer. Can we apply Bergen's theory of multiple affordances to technology? Think back to the Podcast project. Like a jigsaw it appeared to have a specific function but its range of affordances grew the more its use was explored. We could extend its use even further into 'videocasts' where visual and audio elements are combined or lend our voices to creating a virtual world.

Figure 3.2 Web of Technology

In practice, this means ICT can be used to support both adults (staff and parents) and children to promote and implement technology in the EYFS. Look at the Web of Technology diagrams shown in Figures 3.2 and 3.3.

The Early Years Foundation Stage is based around four Themes; each of these is linked to a Principle which in turn is supported by four Commitments which describe how Principles can be put into practice. The Web (Figure 3.2) radiates out from these themes, through each commitment to give ideas of what these might look like in practice. In effect providing technological learning opportunities as well as opportunities for learning and perhaps enhanced motivation to learn (Van Scoter et al., 2001).

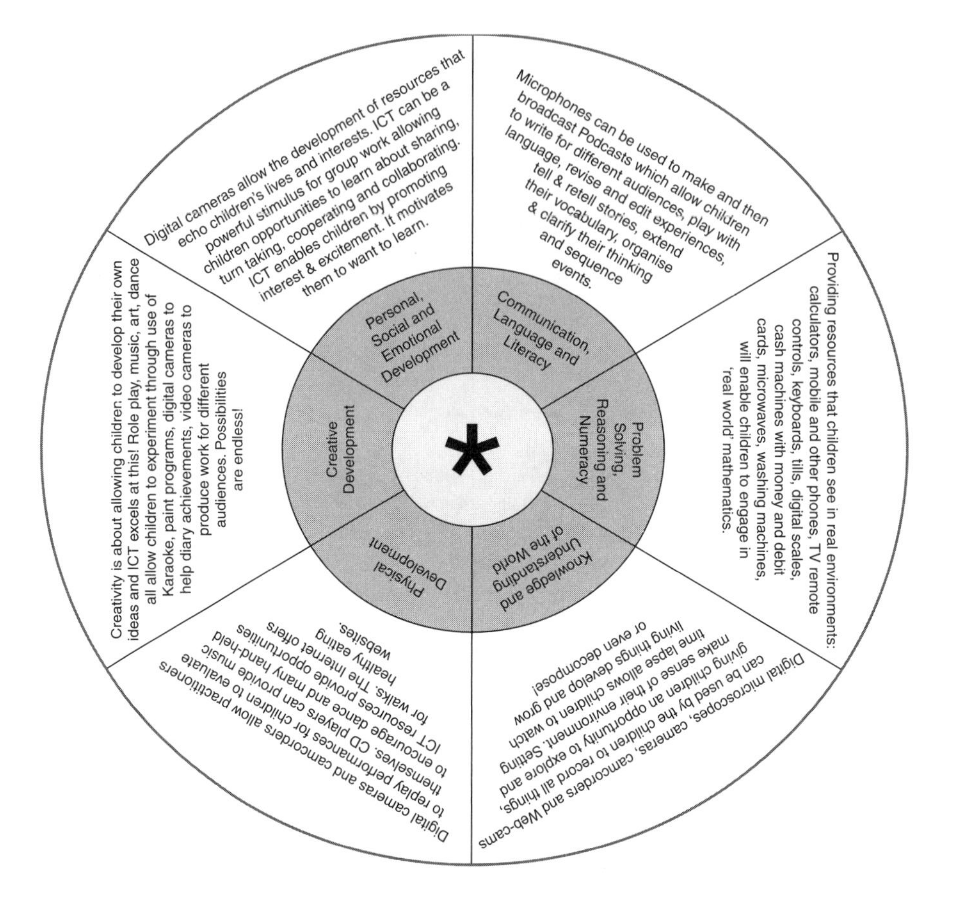

Figure 3.3 How technology can be integrated into each area of the six areas of Learning and Development

A picture of practice – ICT and endless opportunities

The BECTa, award-winning school used in this picture of practice is Lickhill Primary School (formerly Lickhill Lodge First School). It is a local authority maintained foundation school for 4- to 11-year-olds in Worcestershire. All classrooms are equipped with interactive whiteboards and the school is wireless networked so that children use wireless laptops inside and outside the classroom where they also have access to a conservation area, millennium wood, a playground and a shaded role-play area. The school is also involved with the GLOBE programme which is an international environmental education project which encourages children in school to explore and measure their local environment and then makes their findings available to everyone using the Internet.

(Continued)

(Continued)

At Lickhill, a Global Garden which has been developed from an award-winning design by the children is the focus for many aspects of outdoor curriculum work, including data collection for scientists at GLOBE to support research into climate change. This is directly related to providing opportunities for learning in the early years. One aspect of GLOBE is phenology, which encompasses seasonal changes such as bud burst, leaf colour or insect/bird migration. Children observe and record these changes and then enter them into the GLOBE database with adult support. Importantly, this applies to all children at the school. Not just high-flying children and technologically aware staff. The school has a diverse catchment area which includes children who have specific and sometimes challenging needs. The technology therefore has to be 'elastic' allowing entry-level access to those children needing it but 'stretching' those who need to move on through their own exploration of the hardware or software provided.

When you step inside this school, technology is immediately visible. Over the low-level counter in the reception area is a large screen that informs parents about the work their children are doing, through text and pictures, and also notifies them of forthcoming events. Links with families are particularly important and parents can now access examples of their own children's work from home via a password-protected e-portfolio system. They can also listen to children's work via Podcasts and a radio station on the school website. The technology is therefore reasonably sophisticated, however the premise is one that the Office for Standards in Education (Ofsted, 2007) suggests is good practice. In this way the setting keeps parents updated on how their children perform through oral and written information. This e-system lets them share their children's experiences by sometimes allowing them to watch their children's work grow over time. Mobile technologies that motivate and open up endless opportunities to innovate learning and teaching experiences are increasingly available to the children. Importantly, the multi-sensory environment created by the 'Smart boards' allows children to listen, visualise and understand concepts. It is an active and not just a passive agent for learning. It allows children to work collaboratively to develop peer relationships thus improving social skills. This was deemed important in a school that had such a diverse range of abilities within its pupil make-up. This meant considering carefully when and how new digital resources would be used with the children, and ensuring that observation, assessment and planning were clear and based upon the needs of the children, the curriculum focus, and whether the technology chosen would add to children's educational opportunities and experiences.

The results can be seen throughout the school. Staff are more technologically aware, children have visited life underground via a soil safari, discovered giant squids in a virtual submarine, and visited museums and galleries taking virtual tours. They have networked with other settings and other countries, they have used animation and Avatars, made Photostories and video stories.

Point for reflection

- Do you share the view that inclusion of ICT in the early years is necessary to equip children with skills for the future?
- Are you aware of the technology that children are exposed to in their lives? Could you utilise this knowledge to inform future practices? Are you able to keep up to date with technological advances?
- Has the chapter allowed you to think a little more about planning opportunities for learning using ICT?

Summary

Integrating technology, like all work with young children can be challenging but also rewarding. There will always be a lot to learn because while we sometimes struggle with the speed of day-to-day technology changes, global changes are even more dynamic and there will be a need to accommodate these into our practice and children's experiences over time.

Whether it includes a computer or some other type of digital experience technology offers young children unique opportunities for learning through exploration, creativity, problem solving, allowing them to practise, and self-directed instruction. Realising this potential requires a simultaneous focus on curriculum and technology innovations (Hohmann, 1994). Blending technology into the curriculum does demand effort, time, commitment and often a change in our own philosophy. The danger is that by not doing so, we will de-skill our children and leave them ill-prepared for the future.

Useful websites for resources mentioned in this chapter

British Educational Research Association. http://www.bera.ac.uk/
This website provides an overview of some research activities and also offers membership.

British Educational Communications and Technology Agency. http://www.becta.org.uk/
This is a government agency which promotes the use of technology in schools.

Avatar Software. http://www.logitech.com

Avatar software allows children to apply their voice to a different profile, that is, they can talk through a picture of a cat with lips moving and eyes blinking. This allows them to become the cat and talk about their lives, wants and needs – super but simple!

Podium. http://www.podiumpodcasting.com/demos/index.html
Podium offers specific podcasting software for school children and offers video demonstrations to support its use.

http://foundation.e2bn.org/
Foundation Stage specific support for using ICT.

http://www.monsterexchange.com
Offers schools internationally a secure way of networking to improve literacy across the age ranges.

http://www.think.com
A secure social networking site for schools which can run at a local, national or international level.

Some additional useful weblinks

Previous weblinks are directly related to the chapter; however, a more comprehensive list of weblinks for further reading is offered below. In today's digital age, it seems inappropriate to provide further reading from textbooks for a chapter which explores and promotes technology in settings.

The Internet is a fast-moving part of our lives. Websites often change or are adapted in some way. Therefore, the Internet sites shown below are as up to date as possible but may be subject to change as time moves on.

General information and resource sites for ICT and digital technology in the early years

http://www.curriculumonline.gov.uk/

http://www.nwnet.org.uk/

http://www.qca.org.uk/160.html

http://www.surestart.gov.uk/

http://www.mape.org.uk/

http://ngfl.northumberland.gov.uk/

http://www.kented.org.uk/ngfl/earlyict

http://ecs.lewisham.gov.uk/talent/pricor/foundation.html

http://www.northerngrid.co.uk/

http://www.early-education.org.uk/

Sites with practical ideas and resources including video teaching/examples

http://www.kented.org.uk/ngfl/earlyict/
Kent's early years website provides lots of ideas and resources for ICT.

http://www.northerngrid.org/ngflwebsite/eyears.htm
This site is designed by Northern Grid practitioners providing materials for use in the classroom and useful ideas for developing practice.

http://www.teachers.tv/video/3292
A useful video that explores ICT in the early years.

http://www.teachingandlearningtameside.net/index.php?option=com_docman&task=cat_view&gid=88889127&Itemid=88888963
An interesting site that has lots of downloads related to activities and ideas for ICT in the early years.

http://www.ltscotland.org.uk/index.asp
This is the Scottish early years website. It has excellent resources, downloads, ideas and practical support. It is very good for students as many of the articles are free to download. This site contains aspects of theory as well as a focus on practice. Navigate to the ICT early years pages, which are at: http://www.ltscotland.org.uk/earlyyears/resources/publications/ltscotland/index.asp

http://www.ngfl-cymru.org.uk/index-new.htm

This is the Welsh early years website. It provides excellent resources for all key stages and planning ideas are included in the interactive activity files.

http://www.eurotales.eril.net/contents.htm

This is a European project and there are simple versions of many stories, illustrated by children. Each story offers the opportunity to write and print your own version.

http://www.booksforkeeps.co.uk/issues/154/102

This is an interesting website that focuses on literacy and has a section on ICT and electronic media. There are some useful resources and downloads.

http://www.canterbury.ac.uk/education/departments/client/publications/examples/another-101-sn.swf

A useful site more focused on Key Stage 1 and upwards. There are some interesting resources and ideas for working with young children.

http://www.theteachernet.co.uk/primary/ict.htm

The teachernet website offers lots of lively and useful links to other resources and updates on software for use with children.

Interactive sites

http://whiteboardchallenge.wikispaces.com/

An interactive site that has links to teacher tube, it provides video examples of using interactive whiteboards and even has a teach yourself challenge for using a whiteboard. This site is useful for teaching and online examples of practice.

http://matrix.ncsl.org.uk/GMATRIX_23198571_39416509/1235327524006/ebrand/matrix/index.cfm?matrix=161&forcenew=yes

A matrix website that incorporates all aspects of BECTa and its work. In particular, the site offers a self-evaluation process so that you can evaluate your own setting against key standards for ICT in the early years, including leadership and management. The main page can be found at: www.matrix.ncsl.org.uk<http://www.matrix.ncsl.org.uk/>

http://www.nyorks.net/get.html?_Action=GetFile&_Key=Data1502&_Id=274&_Wizard=0&_DontCache=1189411687

This website is for children in the Foundation Stage and Key Stage 1. It provides a useful range of links and sites which may be appropriate for young children to use with and/or without adult support. It covers literacy stories and there are also links to other useful resources for students. The main page can be found at: http://www.n-yorks.net/

Information and research

http://www.ttrb.ac.uk/viewArticle2.aspx?contentId=13314

A 2002 review of a publication from Scotland looking at ICT in the early years and the available literature.

https://swww2.le.ac.uk/departments/beyond-distance-research-alliance/projects/elks_project/ELKSblog/learning-and-technology-world-forum

The University of Leicester link page to a world forum on research and technology.

http://www.futurelab.org.uk/resources/publications-reports-articles/opening-education-reports/Opening-Education-Report1141

Eagle, S., Manches, A., O'Malley, C., Plowman, L. and Sutherland, R. (2008) *Perspectives on Early Years and Digital Technologies*. Futurelab online. The full version of this comprehensive report is available to download in pdf format (50 pages).

http://www.everychildmatters.gov.uk/

The Every Child Matters main website that contains a host of information about many strands of early years practice.

http://www.standards.dcsf.gov.uk/eyfs/

The Early Years Foundation Stage website where you can consider ideas about practice for ICT based on the EYFS framework.

References

British Educational Communications and Technology Agency (BECTa) (2008) 'Government says technology in learning is no longer optional'. http://news.becta.org.uk/display.cfm?resID=37361 (accessed 12.03.2008).

Clark, A. and Moss, P. (2001) *Listening to Young Children: The Mosaic Approach*. London: National Children's Bureau.

Clements, D. and Sarama, J. (2003) 'Strip mining for gold: research and policy in educational technology: a response to fool's gold' (in PDF), *AACE Journal*, 11(1): 7–69. http://www.editlib.org/index.cfm/files/paper_17793.pdf?fuseaction=Reader.DownloadFullText&paper_id=17793 (accessed 03.05.2008).

Cordes, C. and Miller, E. (2000) 'Fool's gold: a critical look at computers in childhood'. http://www.allianceforchildhood.net/projects/computers/computers_reports_fools_gold_download.htm> (accessed 03.05.2008).

Department for Children, Schools and Families (DCSF) (2008) 'Early Years Foundation Stage – everything you need to know'. www.dcsf.gov.uk/publications/eyfs (accessed 26.08.2008).

Department for Education and Skills (DfES) (2003) *ICT and Pedagogy*. London: HMSO.

Donaldson, M. (1986) *Children's Minds*. London: HarperCollins.

Haugland, S.W. (1999) 'What roles should technology play in young children's learning?', *Young Children*, 54(6): 26–32.

Hohmann, C. (1994) 'Staff development practices for integrating technology in early childhood education programs', in J.L. Wright and D.D. Shade (eds), *Young Children: Active Learners in a Technological Age*. Washington, DC: National Association for the Education of Young Children.

Hsi, S. (2006) 'Digital learning and play: a synthesis and elaboration', a paper resulting from a Center for Informal Learning and Schools (CILS) annual meeting, the Bay Area Institute.

Office for Standards in Education (Ofsted) (2007) *Getting on Well: Enjoying, Achieving and Contributing*. London: Ofsted.

Prensky, M. (2008) '"Engage me or enrage me": educating today's "digital native" learners'. http://www.marcprensky.com/speaking/Prensky-SpeakingTopics4.pdf (accessed 12.12.2008).

Saracho, O. and Spodek, N. (2008) *Contemporary Perspectives on Science and Technology in Early Childhood*. Charlotte, NC: Information Age.

Terrific Teaching Solutions (2008) 'Electric education: electrifying learning – Easi Speak'. http://www.electric-education.com/esindex.php (accessed 12.11.2008).

Van Scoter, J., Ellis, D. and Railsback, J. (2001) *Technology in Early Childhood Education: Finding the Balance*. Portland, OR: Northwest Regional Educational Laboratory (NWREL).

Wartella, E.A. and Jennings, N. (2000) 'Children and computers: new techology – old concerns' (in PDF), *The Future of Children: Children and Computer Technology*, 10(2). http://www.futureofchildren.org/information show.htm?doc id=69798 (accessed 01.05.2008).

4

Policy to Practice in Wales

Michael Reed and Alison Morrall

Chapter objectives

This chapter explores policy formation for early years education in Wales. It allows us to examine the way that early education policy has developed leading to the introduction of a new curriculum framework, the Foundation Phase (DCELLS, 2008). It also allows us to understand and reflect upon the notion that education policy and practice is not universally applied in the same way throughout the four nations of the United Kingdom. There are unquestionably differences between the four nations, but there are also significant similarities. Foremost of these is a developing professional and political consensus of ways to support children and families based upon the tenets of *Every Child Matters* (DfES, 2003) and the *Common Core of Skills and Knowledge* (DfES, 2005). In addition, there is currently a developing view that the ability to carefully consider and reflect upon practice is an important professional skill. These skills are part of the whole process of policy formation, change and implementation.

Policy development

A detailed view of the way education policy and practice in Wales has developed in particular over the last decade, is provided by Clark and Waller (2007). They underline how the Welsh Assembly

Government (WAG) has 'quietly established' its own priorities in early education. A significant part of this process has been the gradual implementation of the Foundation Phase curriculum. This has its origins in a document entitled *The Learning Country* which set out the Welsh Assembly Government's education and lifelong learning programme to 2010 (DCELLS, 2001). The Foundation Phase is based on the principle that early years provision should offer a sound foundation for future learning and achievement through a developmentally appropriate curriculum, which is in harmony with the child's particular needs and interests. The underpinning philosophy which forms the basis for the Foundation Phase is the belief that the support and stimulation children receive in their early years fundamentally affects their abilities and potential throughout life.

The Welsh Assembly Government underpinned these aims by indicating their commitment (in the development of policy and their actions) to laying a secure foundation for the education and welfare of young children. The aim was to improve outcomes for the most disadvantaged. They also included a view that childcare was part of the economic fabric of the country and good quality childcare was the aim. For example, the Welsh Assembly Government's 'Childcare Strategy for Wales' (DTA, 2005) aims to support three broad interrelated objectives:

- that all childcare supports the developmental needs of children in Wales;
- that all childcare is widely available and affordable, to enable parents to train or work and thus raise levels of economic activity in Wales;
- that childcare is provided so that parents can have flexibility and choice in how they balance family, work and other commitments within their lives, and in doing so promote gender equality within the workforce.

These aims have been transferred into wider initiatives which include an emphasis upon the 0–3 age group and the Foundation Phase (2008) for 3- to 7-year-olds. They all support the *Learning Country* proposals in 2001 which suggested there is a need to:

- raise children's standards of achievement;
- enhance children's positive attitudes to learning;

- address children's developing needs;
- enable children to benefit from educational opportunities later in their lives;
- help children become active citizens within their communities.

In order to implement these aims, a change of approach and delivery in the classroom and, more significantly, outside the classroom was required. Greater emphasis would be placed on play and active involvement and on the development of children's learning and the acquisition of skills and their application. It was therefore decided to run a pilot to trial the 'Draft Framework for Children's Learning' and its associated guidance material. The pilot began in September 2004 in 41 schools and settings, and it was planned to continue until September 2008 when the statutory rollout was scheduled to begin. However the timescales had to be changed due to a number of factors, including the availability of appropriately trained and skilled adults. The pilot included settings in schools and in voluntary and private nurseries, playgroups and childminders' homes. The evidence gathered during the pilot was evaluated and used to shape the final requirements of the Foundation Phase (2008). This included:

- a play-based and experiential view of learning that involves guided play and learning and interaction with appropriate challenge;
- an appropriate balance between academic and social emotional aims;
- developing literacy skills via an interaction with adults, without formal teaching strategies;
- a common assessment system across all sectors to facilitate children's transitions and family moves;
- an aim to ensure that all settings have similar levels of training, resources and support which would include qualified teacher involvement;
- recommendations regarding the child to adult and teacher ratios;
- clearer roles for local authority staff who would lead the development (DCELLS, 2008).

Point for reflection

The recommendations included aims and objectives about supporting children's well-being. They also encompass important issues such as deciding upon an appropriate ratio of adults to children, the amount of space required for young children to undertake activities and the best teaching and learning strategies for this age group.

- Do you think these are part of the 'essential components' necessary to construct a viable early years framework?
- Do these appear in the framework you are most familiar with?

Coordination

Policy formation and implementation requires significant levels of coordination between different agencies and Wales is no different to other nations in having to do this. The 'Children in Wales' website contains information on many agencies and assists in the coordination of services (Voluntary and Statutory). These include:

- 22 local authorities;
- Early Years Development and Childcare Partnerships (EYDCP);
- Sure Start Partnerships;
- Early Years Forums;
- County Voluntary Councils.

There are also early years task groups, under eights coordinators, Registration and Inspection Officers, Early Years Advisers, as well as the voluntary sector. There are also national networks such as:

- the Flying Start Programme;
- the Integrated Children Centres All-Wales Network;
- the Sure Start Network;
- the Early Years and Childcare Advisory Group (Children in Wales, 2007).

These are often allied to organisations representing a national perspective within the UK such as the Early Childhood Education Forum and the National Family and Parenting Institute.

Quality assurance and monitoring

Early years provision is inspected and reviewed by Eystn, the inspection service in Wales. They inspect nursery schools and settings that are maintained by, or receive funding from, local education authorities (LEAs). The aim of the inspection is to identify the good features and the shortcomings in the provision, which will help settings to improve the quality of education they offer. This will help children to progress in their learning and achieve high standards. Details of the Inspection process and a comprehensive view of inspection arrangements can be viewed by consulting 'Guidance on the inspection of educational provision for children before compulsory school age in settings' (Eystn, 2008). Inspection is seen as an important facet of policy implementation and there has been a concerted effort made to improve practice via the inspection process and disseminate important findings to those most closely involved.

Timing and debate

The Foundation Phase proposals were the subject of debate, intense fiscal planning and extensive consultation. This was not without controversy. Academic commentators, newspapers and other media formats reported how the proposals have been subject to considerable scrutiny. There was debate over the structure of the pilot programme, after it was introduced in 2004. There were murmurings from headteachers over the introduction of the Foundation Phase and some even spoke of boycotting its introduction if adequate funds were not in place. There followed delays over implementation and considerable discussion between policy makers and practitioners over the timing of the changes required to implement the programme. In addition, some commentators felt that the roll-out was not being implemented as planned across all the age groups and pressed for sufficient funds and training to ensure that the principles underpinning the Foundation Phase were implemented fully. For example, the National Day Nurseries Association's *Policy Paper* for Cymru asked that a number of concerns be heeded (NDNA, 2008).

The NDNA (Cymru) were quite vocal in trying to ensure that funding for day-care settings needed to be part of a cohesive approach to childcare availability via integrated children's services. There was also concern from a variety of agencies about pay scales for practitioners, quality assurance schemes and the introduction of training programmes. Many of these criticisms were given attention, but a main block to implementation remained which was the cost of these proposals. However, in June 2008, Jane Hutt, the Minister for Children, Education and Lifelong Learning and Skills, reported an extra £5 million towards the roll-out of the Foundation Phase, which became a statutory requirement for 3- to 4-year-olds from September 2008 (WAG, 2008a). Although this meant implementation would now take place over four years and not three, there was still a commitment to offer a positive early years framework for young children and maintain a 1:8 adult to child ratio for 3- to 5-year-olds (WAG, 2008b). This was an important part of the process of policy implementation and there was now an opportunity to move forward this important agenda for change.

The learning framework

The Foundation Phase has at its core an emphasis upon children's learning, including a drive to improve literacy levels and communication. There is a very powerful focus on play as a fundamental part of how young children learn. There is also a commitment to supporting bilingualism and cultural diversity. The curriculum has been developed under seven areas of learning:

- Personal and Social Development, Well-being and Cultural Diversity;
- Language, Literacy and Communication Skills;
- Mathematical Development;
- Bilingualism;
- Knowledge and Understanding of the World;
- Physical Development;
- Creative Development.

The Foundation Phase places great emphasis on developing children's skills and understanding, including the development of literacy and personal, social, emotional and intellectual well-being. It aims to develop the whole child and underpins positive attitudes and dispositions towards learning so that children enjoy learning and establish a purposeful view of education. This in turn is intended to build upon the development of self-esteem and self-confidence, allowing children to experiment, investigate, learn new things, and form new relationships. It encourages creative and expressive abilities and provides opportunities for children to develop as individuals. They are encouraged to learn by creating an environment which promotes activities indoors and especially outdoors, using first-hand experience of solving problems and how to conserve and sustain the environment. The outdoors is seen as another classroom where children can work on a daily basis. This ethos promotes health and fitness and encourages first-hand experiences of nature. The Foundation Phase therefore places great emphasis on children learning by doing and becoming actively involved in their own learning. It promotes the idea that children need to be motivated to learn. Therefore, speaking, listening, and the development of practical and responsive communication are seen as a solid basis for the development of reading and writing.

Assessment is along a continuum that follows a child from birth to 7 years of age. It is seen as a continuous process of assessment by those most closely involved with the child. Parents and agencies who work with young children and their families, such as Health Visitors and Sure Start workers, will be able to contribute to the 'assessment continuum' before children enter education. The information provided will help staff to prepare an appropriate curriculum for children with an individualised curriculum planned for children who may have difficulties accessing the Foundation Phase framework. It is important to note that the Welsh Assembly Government has made a commitment to creating a bilingual nation where Welsh and English are used equally. To achieve this, it is thought essential that young children have increased opportunities to learn Welsh and to use the language in their everyday activities. This is based on the premise that having two languages helps children to think creatively and flexibly and increases cultural understanding. It should also prepare children for learning other languages. This is seen as increasingly important, as Wales is becoming a multicultural community. Therefore it is stressed that children should learn about different cultures and respect and celebrate diversity from different racial, cultural and religious traditions.

Point for reflection

There are similarities between the Foundation Phase Framework in Wales and the Early Years Foundation Stage (EYFS) (DCSF, 2008), as applied to England. Both see play as a central medium for learning, there is a focus on parental partnership, cultural diversity, literacy and communication as well as the importance of the learning environment and supporting transitions. There are also differences, as EYFS requires all children to be allocated a key worker (staff member) to support their emotional, social and educational well-being. The Foundation Phase Wales focuses on bilingualism (Welsh language). In terms of assessment, the EYFS focuses on identifying the needs of children and there is guidance about planning and recording specific attainments that children should reach. In Wales there is an emphasis on continuous assessment via a qualitative approach that is part of a process which has moved away from formal assessment as a child moves though primary education.

Into practice

The first section of this chapter considered the development of early years policy and the design and development of a curriculum framework in Wales. It revealed a comprehensive regard for the needs of children and a clear message about the value of play, underpinning the principles enshrined in *Every Child Matters*. Of course, these are early days; the curriculum although planned and rolled out over a period of time, has now to be implemented. That implementation falls to the practitioners most closely involved in the process, but also to those colleagues who are part of local authority Early Years Advisory and Support Teams. They have had to manage the process of implementation and steer the framework towards meaningful action in the workplace. They may well be involved in the 'delivery process' or 'delivery models' initiated by central government and usually distributed outwards via a programme of 'capacity building'. This is where training is provided and key issues related to practice cascaded down to those at the 'chalk face'. This usually has targets, aims and objectives and a timescale or chronology of implementation. An examination of the process would tell us something about the structure of implementation and, to an extent, why certain aspects of the curriculum framework are considered important. However, it would not necessarily tell us about how the underlying ethos of the Foundation Phase is being promoted and how practitioners are supported as they strive to implement changes in practice. It would not allow us to reflect on a response to change or tell us about the need for clear and supportive networks that recognise change is a process and not an event. This is because leading change is a complex area of study, and it is much more than putting in place structures and processes. Nothing is more important in the 21st century than learning to manage change (Fullan, 2008).

The management of change also requires leadership in terms of organising and managing early years services. Aubrey (2007) provides a detailed picture of how managers and leaders are responding to change, asking that they are flexible and understand that managing change will be an integral part of their professional lives; a point that Reed (2008) considers in relation to the way differing professional groups are responding to required governmental change in England. A most useful review of the literature focusing on the subject of leadership in the early years was prepared by Dunlop (2008). In addition, there is an interesting perspective on leadership and change written by Murray (2009), who advocates a framework for the development of 'Principled Leadership'. This is seen as an ethical, moral and child-centred approach, understanding your own values and what is understood by effective practice. She suggests that we need to nurture an enabling working environment and apply these values consciously to particular leadership and management situations, challenges, and dilemmas. It is perhaps in this context that the implementation of change and in particular the Foundation Phase should be seen.

A picture of practice

Let us take a snapshot of the 'implementation of policy' in the county of Powys in Wales. Powys is a rural county that has an extensive geographical spread and covers a 'rural' county that encompasses towns and small rural communities. It is the most sparsely populated county in England and Wales, covering some 2000 square miles. The Powys Children and Young People's Plan (2008–2011) says:

> The population on the whole enjoys good health, a high quality natural environment, low crime rates and low unemployment. However underneath this apparent 'rural idyll' there are serious issues impacting on quality of life, health and well being for individuals, families and communities. Due to the rural nature of the county access to

(Continued)

(Continued)

many social, health and other services and facilities are more difficult than in urban areas. Services for children and young people in particular can be affected by the need to provide services to a small population across a large area. (Powys CYPP, 2008: online)

Point for reflection

You may be thinking, why a picture of Powys? Of course, we could have taken our snapshot of practice in an urban area or considered implementation as a whole throughout Wales. However, we wanted to illustrate the way that even in the most geographically challenging areas implementation is taking place. What is more, it is taking place due to the efforts of a motivated team of practitioners who, as we shall see, are taking a considered and reflective view of the Foundation Phase. It is therefore less to do with geographical limitations, more to do with reflection informing and developing the implementation of practice. Of course, we realise that Powys provides only one picture of practice concerning the way a local authority is implementing the Foundation Phase. Therefore it would be unwise to generalise or compare the actions of one local authority to another, and this is not the intention. However, there are areas of what we may call 'general applicability' that we can consider.

The Early Years Team in Powys consists of a number of advisory staff that have a direct and practical influence on the process of implementation. They have embraced new technologies and developed an extensive website which is both interactive and purposeful in the way it supports information exchange. The site is quite responsive to the needs of practitioners as it asks for critical comments about not only training events attended, but also regarding aspects of good practice. It acknowledges and responds to queries and suggestions from its service users and contains the names of officers from the local authority and points of contact. It details available training and feedback from practitioners relating to the quality and relevance of training provided. The team members are very much part of the early years community, travelling extensively to meet practitioners and visit settings. They have all been directly involved in the process of implementing the Foundation Phase, as part of the pilot programme. On occasions they have had to respond to the sometimes difficult process of not knowing if the finance to support

(Continued)

(Continued)

implementation would be forthcoming. They have also had to be adaptable when using generic training materials from the Welsh Assembly Government to ensure that these were presented in a way that reflects the needs of local communities and the specific needs of the settings in their county.

It is important to note that they view themselves as providers of advice and support, seeing their role as more than 'gatekeepers of resources' or indeed the providers of training. They see implementation as 'sharing expertise', maintaining a focus at all times on the 'needs of the children', in particular on 'how children learn'. This places further value on the importance of engaging in small-scale investigations, monitoring the process and assessing the impact on children, aiming to share the results with other practitioners. In terms of underpinning 'reflective practice', it is interesting to note the component parts of the process that the team felt were important. These included:

- Identifying and using good practice. This is interpreted as not only identifying good practice, but using such practice to inform future work, learning from both success and limitations, and to finding ways to share this practice with those most closely involved. This is a view that Karen Appleby in Chapter 1 explores in terms of reflective practice, when she considers the need for 'open exploration' and cites Moon (2007) who sees this as the ability or process of finding out how something is or to find out more about it.
- Adaptability, making things meaningful to all. This was seen as not only being flexible and viewing things from a number of perspectives, but also as being able to identify areas of importance that were attainable, realistic and not needing to be 'perfect'. Again, this is an important part of reflective practice seen by Karen Appleby, who considers the need for critical thinking that is active and deliberate, acknowledging the way actions are perceived by others. Indeed, it could be argued that the team reflected carefully on which aspects of practice they shared in order to make these realistic and purposeful to those involved. In this way, they considered how others perceived them, focusing close attention on their own actions, not just presenting information for others to use.
- Involving people in the process and giving ownership. This was seen as highly important and was the premise behind the use of the website and engaging with practitioners to share expertise. What was interesting was the way the team perceived this as important, but had not necessarily articulated this as such as

(Continued)

(Continued)

part of policy. It was, however, embedded into practice. There was a genuine assumption that if practitioners were asked their views, they would respond and by publishing them (on the web or by sharing good practice at formal training events), they would therefore have a degree of ownership of their ideas and recognise the skills which informed the critical thinking of the team. Practitioners are therefore seen as far more than people holding technocratic skills; they are required to consider, reflect and have varied opinion on practice. Whether this was, a deliberate action to engage others in critical reflection is not clear. However, there is evidence that critical reflection (by selection and action) was apparent in the process. We can also debate if this is part of forming or forging a 'Community of Practice' based around the implementation of the Foundation Phase; the types of communities that Sue Callan, Victoria Cooper and Karen Appleby write about in their chapters – communities that attempt to support others and understand the learning journeys each takes, as well as considering the process of learning experienced by others.

Summary

There are many aspects that could be raised for further discussion, from this short review of policy and practice. For example:

- Is it appropriate to place such a focus on experiential learning into the Foundation Phase?
- What is the importance of viewing culture, language and the environment as essential components of early learning in the principality?

It could be a discussion of the way that policy and the implementation of policy has been forged and managed in Wales compared with the other four nations. It might be about the way this chapter as well as others in this book, has started to identify the way practitioners are reflecting on practice and can critically elaborate on the work they do. These (and no doubt many others) are important aspects. However, this chapter is also addressing something else. It is providing a simple reminder that policy formation is a long-term process. It involves change; change that sometimes will be resisted and sometimes accepted, and change that can be challenged in terms of purpose and content. The chapter also tells us that (regardless of any personal or professional differences) there are reflective practitioners in place that have the welfare of children foremost in their minds, that they are responding to change and attempting to implement policy with the cooperation of

(Continued)

(Continued)

those most closely involved. The chapter represents a snapshot of practice framed by contributions from commentators and policy makers who have generated their own images along the way. The full picture album tells a larger and more complex story about the implementation of the Foundation Phase. We hope you now are more informed about the way policy development has taken place over many years and involved people with vision and any number of dedicated professionals. It tells us that reflective practice has much to do with the way that teams of people compare and contrast what they do and, importantly, are prepared to involve those with a stake in the process. However, we need to remember it provides no more than a starting point to reflect on the intricate nature of policy formation. Inevitably, the Foundation Phase in Wales over time, will be subject to refinement, adaptation, and change. This will involve debate, perhaps argument and certainly changes in direction and even changes in policy. It will require people to reflect on the whole process and as a result change practice. Therefore, we say again, this is only a snapshot, however, we hope it will encourage you to have a more considered view of the process of change, to compare and contrast action from one of the 'other' four nations of the UK, and start to reflect on that process.

Suggested further reading

- Clark, M. M. and Waller, T. (eds) (2007) *Early Childhood Education and Care: Policy and Practice.* London: Sage Publications.
  This book provides a good overview of policy dimensions throughout the UK.

- Murray, J. (2009) 'Value based leadership and management', in A. Robins and S. Callan (eds), *Managing Early Years Settings.* London: Sage Publications.
  This chapter considers the nature and characteristics of early years provision and the influence and demands this might have on the leadership and management of settings.

- Welsh Assembly Government. www.wales.gov.uk/foundationphase
  This chapter is about policy and change. The subject is so new that no books exist about the Welsh Foundation Phase, but you can download 'Learning in the Foundation Phase: A Guide for Parents and Carers. A new approach to the education and care of 3-7 year olds' from the website.

References

Aubrey, C. (2007) *Leading and Managing in the Early Years.* London: Sage Publications.

Children in Wales (2007) 'Areas of work: early years'. http:// www.childreninwales.org.uk/areasofwork/earlyyears/index.html (accessed 23.01.2009).

Clark, M.M. and Waller, T. (eds) (2007) *Early Childhood Education and Care: Policy and Practice*. London: Sage Publications.

Department for Children, Education, Lifelong Learning and Skills (DCELLS) (2001) *Policy Unit Briefing Paper 22 – The Learning Country: A Comprehensive Education and Lifelong Learning Programme to 2010*. Cardiff: National Assembly for Wales DCELLS.

Department for Children, Education, Lifelong Learning and Skills (DCELLS) (2008) *Foundation Phase: Framework for Children's Learning for 3-to 7-year-olds in Wales*. Cardiff: DCELLS.

Department for Children, Schools and Families (DCSF) (2008) *Practice Guidance for the Early Years Foundation Stage*. Nottingham: DCFS.

Department for Education and Skills (DfES) (2003) *Every Child Matters: Change for Children*. Nottingham: DfES.

Department for Education and Skills (DfES) (2005) *Common Core of Skills and Knowledge for the Children's Workforce*. Nottingham: DfES.

Department for Training and Education (DTA) (2005) 'The Childcare Strategy for Wales: Childcare is for Children', DfTE Information Document No. 047-05, November. www.learning.wales.gov.uk (accessed 18.01.2009).

Dunlop, A.W. (2008) 'A literature review on leadership in the early years', University Of Strathclyde – Online Learning and Teaching Scotland. http://www.ltscotland.org.uk/earlyyears/resources/publications/resourcesresearch/leadershipreview.asp (accessed 18.01.2009).

Eystn (2008) 'Guidance on the inspection of educational provision for children before compulsory school age in settings'. www.estyn.gov.uk/home.asp (accessed 06.01.2009).

Fullan, M. (2008) *The Six Secrets of Change*. London: John Wiley and Sons.

Moon, J. (2007) *Critical Thinking: An Exploration of Theory and Practice*. London: Routledge.

Murray, J. (2009) 'Value based leadership and management', in A. Robins and S. Callan (eds), *Managing Early Years Settings*. London: Sage Publications.

National Day Nurseries Association (NDNA) (2008) *Policy Paper – Cymru – June 2008*. Denbighshire: NDNA Cymru.

Powys: Children and Young People's Partnership (CYPP) (2008) *Summary of Powys' Children and Young People's Plan 2008–2011*. www.cypp.powys.gov.uk (accessed 08.09.2009).

Reed, M. (2008) 'Professional development through reflective practice', in A. Paige-Smith and A. Craft (eds), *Developing Reflective Practice in the Early Years*. Maidenhead: Open University Press.

Welsh Assembly Government (WAG) (2008a) *Foundation Phase update – June 2008*. Written statement from the Welsh Assembly Government – Jane Hutt, Minister for Children, Education, Lifelong Learning and Skills.

Welsh Assembly Government (WAG) (2008b) 'Children and young people's well-being monitor for Wales'. www.wales.gov.uk/research (accessed 18.01.2009).

Section 2

The Unique Child

5

Safeguarding Children: Every Child Matters so Everybody Matters!

Claire Majella Richards

Chapter objectives

This chapter underlines the importance of safeguarding children and suggests that it is an essential part of every practitioner's role and responsibility. It asks that we look beyond the environment of the setting and consider the importance of working effectively with parents and families. It also considers the 'new' roles and responsibilities of those leading early years settings. This includes the need to be confident and competent in working in partnership with other professionals and agencies; working together to safeguard children. There is a need to highlight the advocacy role of the practitioner for children's empowerment and the importance of reflective practice.
In doing so, there is allowance for key issues to be identified in order to reflect on practical ways and interventions to support children's welfare.

Terminology

The terms **safeguarding** and **child protection** will be used throughout this chapter and it is useful to explore both concepts. Firstly, child protection; a child's safety and welfare is of paramount importance to all concerned with their world. Therefore, child protection procedures are the main driving force upon which professionals should act when a child is identified as suffering or being at risk of suffering significant harm through abuse and neglect. Safeguarding children is about the processes of supporting families and empowering children. It is about early intervention and preventative strategies to ensure better outcomes for children: being safer, more resilient and to grow in confidence, fulfilling their potential.

Policy and the legislative framework: setting the scene

It is poignant to note that the birth of the *Every Child Matters* (ECM) policy in 2004 was borne from the tragic plight of Victoria Climbié, whose short life was brutally diminished in 2000, by the hands of her entrusted carer(s) (Laming Report, 2003). The cruel death of Baby Peter in 2007, a 17-month-old boy who was originally identified by a solitary initial, Baby P, is yet another reminder for everyone of the considerable risk and harm some adults as parents or carers, pose to their children. Both children's names will be a constant reminder to professionals of the shortfalls and failings that can occur in relation to the protection of the welfare of children. More recently, the abuse and suffering of Baby P caused further public outcry and, consequently, again prompted a response from Government. The lessons to be learnt in the wake of this tragedy echo loudly of the case of Victoria. Rightly, there is a focus on holding parents or carers to account for their actions or non-actions in caring for their children. However, there is renewed emphasis and reminders to ensure that professionals and agencies work more effectively together to protect vulnerable children within their local communities.

The recent decade has witnessed a plethora of legislative and policy developments which could have a head-spinning impact on the most skilled practitioner. The pathway of legislation and policy in the wake of Victoria's death and the Laming Report has paved a foundation and framework of reference, guidance and instruction as to the roles and responsibilities of professionals in the context of protecting and safeguarding children. The *Every Child Matters* policy and Children Act 2004 emphasise three of the most important developments from an interagency perspective to protect and safeguard children:

- the creation of children's trusts under the duty to cooperate;
- the setting up of Local Safeguarding Children's Boards (LSCBs);
- the duty on all agencies to make arrangements to safeguard and promote the welfare of children (HM Government, 2006: 10).

These points underline an increasing shift of emphasis on the collective responsibility of professionals and agencies in meeting their requirements to work efficiently and proactively in safeguarding children. Indeed, both safeguarding and interagency working are two of the six key areas of skills and knowledge required of everyone working with children, young people and families via *The Common Core of Skills and Knowledge* (DfES, 2005). In addition, the Government has launched its 10-year vision for children, as the Department for Children, Schools and Families (DCSF) will deliver *The Children's Plan* (2007) promoting the outcomes of the ECM agenda, increasing a more holistic approach in working with parents and families (DCSF, 2007).

These initiatives are embedded within the Early Years Foundation Stage (EYFS) whose principles of welfare and care were paralleled in the Childcare Act 2006 (DCSF, 2008). Both of these new provisions mean that the ECM agenda is reinforced with the aim of ensuring that children do get the best possible start in life; that existing inequalities of life experiences and opportunities are reduced; and service providers are effectively monitored and assessed, with more emphasis on partnerships with parents and families. There is also a continuing focus on early intervention, where the recognition of a child in need instigates the implementation of responsive services for the child's best interests; this may also include a child in need of protection, who has been identified, as a consequence of this assessment process.

Indeed the focus on early intervention continues with the introduction of the Common Assessment Framework (CAF) (CWDC, 2007). It heralded a new era in the culture of working together, insisting on clearer channels of communication between professionals, better accountability and, critically, the recognition and empowerment of the voice of the child and family, as part of this assessment process. The input of the Early Years practitioner to the CAF experience of children and their families is essential to ensuring that the child's best interests are heeded and acted upon. This professional, perhaps more so than any other, has greater contact with the child and has insight to the child's well-being, on a daily basis outside the family home.

Point for reflection

- How important is it that all Early Years practitioners have a clear understanding of the legal and policy frameworks in the context of safeguarding and protecting children?
- Should they all be working to the same frameworks, the same values and principles?
- Is it important that safeguarding and protecting children is securely embedded within all aspects of the curriculum, professional training and the way professional support is given to parents?
- Is this the start of a process of professional and legislative transformation to help us protect the welfare of children?

If you are uncertain about the legal and policy frameworks as well as the processes and procedures would you know where to find this information? (Look at the weblinks at the end of this chapter.)

Working together – a shared responsibility

An Early Years practitioner may be in one of many settings who fall under the provisions of the Children Act 1989. These include private, voluntary and local authority providers for children under the age of 8. They must be registered by Ofsted and should have written procedures based on *What To Do If You Are Worried A Child Is Being Abused – Summary* (DfES, 2006). These procedures should give clear guidance to all staff, including volunteers, about their roles and responsibilities when responding to concerns about suspected child abuse and neglect, in accordance with the outlined procedures and inter-agency guidance of the Local Safeguarding Children Board. This includes the input of the 'Designated Safeguarding Officer' or 'Professional' within the setting whose role is specific to the safeguarding responsibilities of children, promoting leadership and direction for staff in their arrangements to protect children.

For all agencies and professionals working together to safeguard children it is imperative that the child's safety and welfare remains of paramount focus and importance, while those individuals who pose a risk to children are held accountable and monitored effectively to reduce and prevent this harm. Therefore all agencies and professionals should:

- be alert to potential indicators of abuse or neglect;
- be alert to the risks that individual abusers, or potential abusers, may pose to children;
- share and help analyse information so that an assessment can be made of the child's needs and circumstances;
- contribute to whatever actions are needed to safeguard and promote the child's welfare;
- take part in regularly reviewing the outcomes for the child against specific plans;
- work cooperatively with parents, unless this is inconsistent with ensuring the child's safety (HM Government, 2006: 34).

These may seem quite straightforward and easy to assimilate and understand. However, it is rare that such factors are easy or straightforward to implement. For example, Parton (2006: 80) cites Sinclair et al. (1997) by imaginatively describing the journey of childhood – infant to adolescent – as a snakes and ladders board:

> where the ladders represented positive supports and enablers, while the snakes were the mishaps, mistreatment and miseries along the way. The role of preventive services was to provide more ladders and remove or minimise the snakes and their impact.

Parton adds that the role of preventative services, that is, agencies working effectively together, was not just a limited focus to combat risk and negative impact. It moves beyond this stance to maximising the potential and opportunity of protective factors for children; a point that a lay person might see as completely self-evident and hence wonder at the apparent lack of common sense of professional groups and their responses to child protection concerns. Yet, in spite of that common-sense view, our professional heritage reminds us of collective failures of agencies in meeting their single and shared responsibilities to protect vulnerable children. The anxieties and confusion in sharing information about children and families, the prevalence of professional hierarchies and misconceptions of organisational cultures have a part to play in the doubts about role expectations of professionals. This is compounded by misunderstandings of jargon, alienating language communicated by professional groups in meetings or correspondence with other agencies and more perplexing, with families.

Indeed, this was one of the criticisms by Lord Laming (2003) of his inquiry into the death of Victoria Climbié, where there was a pattern of professionals' unwillingness to challenge the opinions of other professionals within a perceived hierarchy. For example, consider the following scenarios where a staff nurse does not question the view of a consultant paediatrician, or a police officer who does not assert her assessment of a potentially dangerous offender to her chief inspector, or the Early Years Professional (EYP) who does not challenge the decision of the chairperson of a case conference about a child protection concern. This point is perhaps best illustrated in the Westminster Serious Case Review (Lock, 2006) following the death of a child, where professional optimism about the safety and welfare of the child being returned to the parental home overshadowed the concerns of the foster parents about the inappropriateness of that decision.

These examples raise issues which are pertinent in light of the national drive to professionalise training of the Early Years workforce, as the Children's Workforce Development Council (CWDC) reviews its own strategy and programme following the Baby Peter case. Sue Callan considers in her chapter and Michael Reed also considers in another chapter, the changes which have led to the formation of children's centres. It is hoped that the new professional holding the status of EYP can stand with confidence and assertion, shoulder to shoulder as a fledgling professional amongst the more established range of professionals, historically working with child protection concerns. The Early Years Professional is a new concept and perhaps not yet widely appreciated or understood by more established professional groups. It would be naive to assume that this new ranking of professional is met with open arms within more established professional networks. In one sense, there is much to prove about matters of professional credibility, competence and confidence. A point that Wendy Messenger discusses in her chapter on considering the professional qualities needed for interagency working. What is important, is to try to shed some of our professional inhibitions about differing roles, experience and training and to assert professionalism through the voice of the child; to be an advocate for the child, speaking in the context of our professional knowledge and experience of the child and family; to consider how we might speak with true authority and insight as to what it is like or may be like to be in a particular child's shoes, in that particular child's world.

Level of Need	Children's Needs	Access to Professional Support and Intervention
Level 4	The child has experienced significant harm and requires more intensive support from agencies.	Examples include child protection procedures, looked after children or residential or secure accommodation in the case of older children.
Level 3	This will include the child with complex health and developmental needs, which will deteriorate without timely intervention.	Child and Adolescent Mental Health Services and Children's Integrated Area Services.
Level 2	The child's health and development may be adversely affected without intervention and is at risk of not meeting their full potential.	Common Assessment Framework and support links through Children's Centres, Specialist Speech and Language Services or other aspects of health-related provision.
Level 1	Where the needs of the child can be met through universal services without the need for additional support.	Health visitor, school nurse, school environment, GP, leisure facilities and early years setting.

Figure 5.1 Child's needs and access to professional support and interventions

Children may need the help of professionals at various points in their development, whether this is for a speech and language delay, a behavioural difficulty or grieving the loss of a parent or family member. These access points to help, likely to have been initiated by a parent or with the support of another professional such as a health visitor or general practitioner (GP), can be both timely and time limited. Subsequent referrals or access points to help for intensive support for more complex needs are identified as secondary and tertiary level interventions (Krug et al., 2002) and this approach is developed further as a theme by the CAF process. The latter describes different levels or tiers of interventions and examples of stepping up to more intensive service provision for a child and family with more complex needs.

Working together in itself may be a worthwhile aim. It may prompt a quicker response to a more rounded and informed view of a problem. Nevertheless, it still means that a professional has to make their decision as to when to intervene or contact another agency. They may find themselves recognising the occasions when a parent may struggle and ask for help. This inevitably creates a dilemma. The plea for help or disclosure may be inspired by a trust and confidence which has enabled a parent to share his concerns and to seek advice. Such trust and confidence may be difficult to develop and something that may have to be overridden if the issues impact upon the need to protect a child. There is also the case where to seek consent to share information about concerns in order to gain the advice and assistance of other professionals, would place that child at increased risk of harm. In addition to the danger, Howe (2006: 232) suggests:

> Many parents most at risk of seriously maltreating their children are those most likely to avoid and disengage from all types of health and welfare services and interventions.

Further to this, add the possibility of a vulnerable adult within the child's world, in the case, for example, where a mother is being abused by her partner and hence fearful of expressions of concern and offers of help. When engaging and listening to parents, and discussing concerns, the EYP must have continued regard for safeguarding and promoting the welfare of the child who may be living in particularly stressful conditions. This would include:

- living in poverty;
- a concern about domestic abuse;
- a parent with a mental health problem;
- where a parent is misusing drugs or alcohol;
- a parent with a learning disability;
- experiences of racism and social isolation;
- living in an area of high crime, poor housing and high unemployment (HM Government, 2006: 17).

This tells us that there are wide-ranging and complex issues which those leading or managing a setting may have to encounter and address, which are difficult and require expertise, and sensitive and informed ways of working. These can be complex dilemmas but there is a realisation that having a focused and preventative view of safeguarding children's welfare, and a positive view of professional collaborative working together, is a means of a way forward.

Point for reflection

- What qualities does a capable, confident and effective practitioner who positively safeguards the welfare of children require?

The answer may include being:

Knowledgeable, able to solve problems, inquisitive, intuitive, responsive, compassionate, observant, able to assimilate, record and report information quickly and competently, able to forge positive relationships with parents and other professionals, critical, analytical, persistent, assertive, respectful, thoughtful, empathic, insightful, motivated, articulate, confident, competent, active listener, understands what being an advocate means, prioritises issues and is reflective.

The list may cause us to think about the complex and varied role of the Early Years Professional.

- Can you add more qualities to this list?

Beyond policy to positive practice

The Common Core of Skills and Knowledge (DfES, 2005) prescribed for the Children's Workforce underpins key aspects of knowledge and skills required by each practitioner. This is in terms of qualifications and continuing professional development and effectively meeting the needs of children, young people and their families. The skills and knowledge are described under six main headings:

- effective communication and engagement with children, young people and families;
- child and young person development;
- safeguarding and promoting the welfare of the child;
- supporting transitions;
- multi-agency working;
- sharing information.

Each skill is integral to the other and no skill is given greater or lesser emphasis, indeed they should be seen as interrelated rather than mutually exclusive. This working interdependence reminds the reflective and skilled Early Years Practitioner of the holistic approach to understanding the child's world. Yet, critically, there may be aspects of the holistic approach which create a picture that is fragmented or less clear. For example, the practitioner has a sound understanding of the process and uniqueness of the child's development, and he is sensitive to the child's emotional support needs in terms of transition from home to an unfamiliar pre-school setting. However, there may be matters in relation to the child's communication or behaviour which present immediate worry to the practitioner and which are further exacerbated by the difficulty in communicating with the child's parent or carer. For example, the parent may be dismissive of the concerns raised by the practitioner, show evidence of poor emotional self-control or tend to avoid opportunities to listen to or discuss concerns raised by staff within the setting. These features may or may not have links to the safeguarding and promoting of the child's welfare priority and there may be no obvious signs of abuse or neglect of the child. However, the practitioner will still need to take heed of those internally registered concerns and verbalise these observations and experiences with the Designated Safeguarding Officer (DSO) within the setting. A record of observations of the child and subsequent discussion with the DSO, including agreed actions are imperative. This would need to follow a decision by the Practice Manager or DSO to talk to the child's parents about an injury or worrying change in the child's behaviour, and good practice would encourage the practitioner to record parents' explanations or responses. It may be useful and reassuring to discuss a concern, without a full disclosure of personal data with the local authority's Children's Social Care team, in order to get another professional perspective on the concern and what to do if there appears to be a risk to a child.

If a practitioner decides on the basis of their assessment and discussion with the DSO that a child is suffering or is at risk of suffering significant harm, a referral should be made to Children's Social Care immediately. It would be remiss not to acknowledge the personal angst this causes to any professional, not least the professional practitioner who may have a close working relationship with that family. This is a difficult discussion, requiring some degree of personal and professional preparation. Parents should be informed about the referral but a critical decision not to inform a parent may be necessary if to do so would place that child at further risk of significant harm, places an adult at risk of serious harm or would jeopardise a criminal investigation. This again, causes us to consider the professional knowledge and skills required to work effectively in a safeguarding role with parents and other agencies.

These skills will certainly be gained via experience, but will also be gained via training as part of Continuing Professional Development (CPD). This can promote an awareness and ethos of working collaboratively with other agencies, including a respect for all aspects of diversity, such as race, culture and disability. Training emphasises the importance of a child-centred approach, empowering the child and promoting the participation of children and their families in the safeguarding process (HM Government, 2006). However, staff training, no matter how effective or proficient, is of little use in a setting with poor leadership and management of the professional role in safeguarding children. Similarly, perfectly drafted child protection policies are of little professional value if staff are unaware of this provision or the policy procedures in safeguarding children within the setting. There is an important demand on Early Years providers to ensure that the staff team is committed to professional approaches which assuredly promote the safeguarding of children and working with families and other professionals.

It is now clear that every professional, who works with children and has contact with parents, carers or other significant adults connected to the child, should be alert to issues of change or concern which may have some bearing in the context of the child's health and welfare. It is also important to have the ability to reflect and critically examine the needs of families and the child within the family. This is particularly true when focusing on the child's development and the child's voice; listening to and responding to the needs of the child. The practitioner in his or her workplace needs to be vigilant and has a safeguarding remit in terms of the child's well-being; their expressions, actions and reactions to other children and adults. This includes the wider welfare statutory requirements as stipulated by the Early Years Foundation Stage, such as current safe recruitment practices to ensure the employment of suitable and appropriate staff via an enhanced Criminal Records Bureau (CRB) Disclosure, which involves the Protection of Children Act 1999 list, and List 99 consisting of a list of people considered unsuitable to work with children held by the Department for Children, Schools and Families. This scrutiny provides further assurance of the appropriate candidacy of staff that work with children and are likely to have unsupervised access to children. From October 2009, a new scheme governed by the Independent Safeguarding Authority (ISA) stipulates that employers will only be allowed to recruit people who are ISA registered, that is, assessed as not posing a risk to children or vulnerable adults.

The effective Early Years practitioner will be mindful of his/her role in meeting the other welfare requirements of the EYFS, and the wholeness of this approach is represented in those aspects of providing a safe environment for children, equipment and resources. The critical focus on the organisation of the early years setting means that the ethos and care management processes do much to guarantee a quality service of inclusiveness. A respectfulness of the diversity of children and their families, including a commitment to celebrate and promote the uniqueness and potential of every child through key worker systems and child-led initiatives, do much to promote systems and approaches which are child rooted and child empowering. Scrupulous documentation and record-keeping systems are a necessity too, and will complement those organisational approaches in place. Access and provision of accurate and meaningful data about children, including records and observations, may have a critical input in terms of evidence-based decisions and actions in relation to safeguarding and child protection procedures.

Summary

This chapter has considered critical professional issues in the realm of safeguarding and protecting children. There has been a necessary focus on the emerging recognition and broader promotion of safeguarding as a consensus throughout all aspects of childcare in the United Kingdom. More recently this has been firmly underlined as part of all professional training and is embedded in the role of the EYP especially in terms of working with other agencies to safeguard children. No doubt, the ongoing development of children's centres in playing a pivotal role in the provision of services for children and their families will include a growing awareness and poly-professional recognition of safeguarding the welfare of children.

Today there is an expectation that the proactive and reflective practitioner is mindful of his or her role in ensuring observations and professional judgements are evidence-based and child-rooted. They need to work collaboratively with parents and follow procedures stipulated by the statutory requirements of their setting and as indicated by the procedures of the Local Safeguarding Children Board. Crucially, they need to have an understanding that in promoting the welfare of children in their care, no single agency or professional can address child protection or safeguarding in isolation. It truly is a matter of working together; as every child matters, so everybody matters. It is also a matter of developing the ability to reflect on their own practice. When this happens they are truly moving towards the view that if every child matters, then everyone has a responsibility to make sure they do.

Suggested further reading

- Cleaver, H., Unell, I. and Aldgate, J. (1999) *Children's Needs – Parenting Capacity. The Impact of Parental Mental Illness, Problem Alcohol and Drug Use, and Domestic Violence on Children's Development.* London: TSO.
  This text provides an effective overview of some critical issues that may have a significant impact on parenting capacity, supporting parents and the implications for children.

- Department for Children, Schools and Families (DCSF) (2008) *Staying Safe: Action Plan.* Nottingham: DCSF.
  Government strategy on improving children's safety and new commitments for the next three years.

- Department for Education and Skills (DfES) (2006) *What To Do If You Are Worried A Child Is Being Abused – Summary.* Nottingham: DfES.
  A practice guidance to assist practitioners to work together to safeguard and promote children's welfare.

Useful websites

All of the government websites below will provide further information in the context of the safeguarding issues highlighted within this chapter.

Every Child Matters:
http://www.everychildmatters.gov.uk/
http://www.everychildmatters.gov.uk/safeguarding
http://www.everychildmatters.gov.uk/informationsharing
http://www.everychildmatters.gov.uk/commoncore/

Independent Safeguarding Authority: http://www.isa-gov.org

Victoria Climbié Inquiry: http://www.victoria-climbie-inquiry.org.uk/finreport/finereport.htm

References

Children's Workforce Development Council (CWDC) (2007) *Common Assessment Framework for Children and Young People: Practitioners Guide.* London: CWDC.

Department for Children, Schools and Families (DCSF) (2007) *The Children's Plan: Building Brighter Futures.* London: HMSO.

Department for Children, Schools and Families (DCSF) (2008) *Practice Guidance for the Early Years Foundation Stage.* Nottingham: DCSF.

Department for Education and Skills (DfES) (2005) *The Common Core of Skills and Knowledge for the Children's Workforce.* Nottingham: DfES.

Department for Education and Skills (DfES) (2006) *What To Do If You Are Worried A Child Is Being Abused – Summary.* Nottingham: DfES.

HM Government (2006) *Working Together to Safeguard Children. A Guide to Inter-agency Working to Safeguard and Promote the Welfare of Children.* London: HMSO.

Howe, D. (2006) *Child Abuse and Neglect, Attachment, Development and Intervention.* Basingstoke: Palgrave Macmillan.

Krug, E.G., Dahlberg, L.L., Mercy, J.A., Zwi, A.B. and Lozano, R. (2002) *World Report on Violence and Health.* Geneva: World Health Organisation.

Laming Report (2003) *The Victoria Climbiè Inquiry: Report of an Inquiry by Lord Laming.* London: HMSO.

Lock, R. (2006) *Serious Case Review, Executive Summary.* Westminster Local Safeguarding Children Board, 22 August.

Parton, N. (2006) *Safeguarding Childhood, Early Intervention and Surveillance in a Late Modern Society.* London: Palgrave Macmillan.

6

A Healthy Child – Direction, Deficit or Diversity?

Mandy Andrews and Kate Fowler

Chapter objectives

This chapter explores concepts of health and attempts to understand what is meant by a 'Healthy Child'. It suggests that a reflective, informed and critically aware practitioner can have a profound effect on children's well-being. However, to do this, they need to define and perhaps refine what they consider to be a 'healthy child'.

It considers the following questions:

- Why is it important to support child health?
- What it meant by child health and well-being?
- What can be learnt from the experiences of others?

> The true measure of a nation's standing is how well it attends to its children – their health and safety, their material security, their education and socialisation, and their sense of being loved, valued and included in the families and societies into which they are born. (UNICEF, 2007: 1)

Why is it important to consider and support child health?

In relation to *The Children's Plan* 2007 the DCSF underlines the point that 'Improving children's health is important for everyone – for families, communities and Government' (DCSF, 2007: online). Children are the future of society, the next generation of workers, entrepreneurs, thinkers, inventors and future parents. It can be argued that a healthy childhood allows children and young people to make the most of opportunities in life. Conversely, poor health, physical and emotional can be a barrier to enjoying life and fulfilling potential. These are the tenets that drive forward our view of developing a healthy child, which were recognised by Maslow (1943: 380). He suggested people had basic needs, such as food, shelter, love and belonging, all effectively health needs. He argued that these needed to be in place to support higher-level thinking skills and an achievement that he termed 'self-actualisation'. This can be illustrated by thinking about a time when a person has experienced lack of concentration due to hunger, cold, or illness. At these times it may be difficult to focus on basic needs, let alone mental exploration and understanding. Such simple common experiences allow us to understand that 'Children learn best when they are healthy, safe and secure, when their individual needs are met and they have positive relationships' (DCSF, 2008c: 14).

How healthy are children today?

The National Service Framework of 2004 stated that 'Children and young people in Britain enjoy better health than any previous generation' (DoH, 2004: 4). A UNICEF report on children's well-being, compared child well-being internationally and identified that children are experiencing, 'an historically unheard of level of health' pointing out that: 'whilst almost within living memory, one child in every five in the cities of Europe could be expected to die before his or her fifth birthday; today that risk is less than one in a hundred'. The report went on to say that 'overall, approximately 80% of young people consider their health to be good or excellent in every OECD country (except the United Kingdom)' (UNICEF, 2007: 13).

If it is true that the health of children is indicative of the state of the country, perhaps despite the successes outlined above, there is cause for concern. In 2006 Sue Palmer generated an international debate with her book *Toxic Childhood* when she argued that 'Instead of building healthy bodies [we are] simply making children fatter and unhealthier by the year' (Palmer, 2006: 21). She cited evidence that children in developed (Western European) countries are today more likely to suffer illnesses brought on by poor diet and lack of exercise, and are more likely to suffer from mental health problems than previous generations (Palmer, 2006: 27). Albon and Mukherji, (2008) reinforce this point and indicate concern over diet and health. The UK Government has also recognised that 'we are facing pressing public health priorities such as the rise in childhood obesity, an increase in emotional and behavioural problems among children and young people, and the poor outcomes experienced by children in the most at-risk families' (Shribman, 2007: 8).

The 2007 UNICEF report used standard measures of child health at birth, child immunisation rates and deaths from accidents and injuries, and found that there were quite significant inequities in child health experiences between nations. Whilst the countries ranking highest were largely the European countries, the United Kingdom lagged behind some which may be considered to be less developed (UNICEF, 2007). They also found that the specific measure of infant mortality rates ranged from under 3 deaths per 1,000 births in Iceland and Japan to over 6 per 1,000 in the more affluent United States, and they further found that 'If all OECD countries had the same child injury death rate as Sweden ... then approximately 12,000 child deaths a year could be prevented' (UNICEF, 2007: 22).

It is evident that whereas affluence and absence of poverty had been generally linked to good child health outcomes in the past, they were now not necessarily a true indicator of potential health. In some cases, greater affluence is having a negative impact on health through lack of exercise and poor nutrition. This understanding is more recently reflected in the development of Sure Start Children's Centres supporting families in all areas, not just those targeted areas of deprivation identified for the initial delivery of Sure Start Local Programmes.

Point for reflection

As early childhood professionals you are probably able to access a range of conflicting data as exemplified above. You are also presented with a range of government directives and legislative guidance. It is now possible to do online searches and identify new or current research information about health issues. Take time to seek out new information and update your understanding. Then reflect and consider what this means for the way that you work with 'your' children. What actions may you take as a result of this reflection?

A picture of practice at a Sure Start children's centre

An *Every Child Matters* target is the reduction of obesity (DCSF, 2008b). The examples come from the work of practitioners in two different children's centres. Both centres are involved in promoting healthy eating and reducing obesity. They demonstrate an individual approach to the same subject, influenced by a particular local context.

> We realised from conversations and experience that many families in our area were eating ready meals. Statistics and early research identified that dental health and obesity issues existed in the area in adults and children. We had requested a dental service from our Children's Centre. At the same time a local 'Veggie Box' scheme was being developed (selling local produce at affordable prices and reducing packaging costs for the producer). The 'Veggie Box' scheme enabled us to address the healthy eating issues we had identified. Boxes of fresh vegetables were offered to families at a subsidised price.
>
> We found we needed to reflect again as we overheard parents saying that they did not know how to cook with the fresh vegetables offered in the box, despite the inclusion of a recipe card. Realising that the inclusion of a recipe card was not enough we were able, as a children's centre to offer cookery classes for parents and their children. In this way parents learnt how to cook with fresh food and children were able to also learn future cookery skills and healthy eating habits in the company of their parent. We interpreted the guidance and wait to see if the statistics change as a result, but probably won't really see the impact until the next generation of parents! (Children's Centre Worker)
>
> We have to be aware of, and respond to new guidance all the time. Being Healthy does relate to food and healthy eating and that provides an example of practice for us. We used to offer drinks and biscuits. Over

(Continued)

(Continued)

the years as a result of guidance we have shifted to offer more healthy snack times. As we learn more we have continually weighed things up and refined our thinking about child health. For example, we quite recently offered dried fruit as a snack, but then we became aware of the high sugar content, so we now only offer fresh fruit. It is important that we keep up to date, but also respond to our children's needs, such as cultural needs. (Nicki Ovel and Linda Picken – Children's Centre Childcare Managers, Merry-Go-Round Nursery, Hereford)

Perhaps it is in part because this is both a limited view of health, and is obviously interpreted locally that Lajole and Leveille (2007) are able to be critical of the UNICEF report by suggesting 'Child well being is a multi dimensional concept that is difficult to measure and even more difficult to compare' (Lajole and Leveille, 2007: 4). They go on to state that some indicators of health and well-being are simply unavailable, such as exposure to domestic violence, mental health and emotional well-being. Whilst most governments have agreed that it is a fundamental right of every child to be supported to 'the enjoyment of the highest attainable standard of health and to facilities for the treatment of illness and rehabilitation of health' (UNICEF, 1990: 8), exactly what this looks like is not clear. Government directives often focus on those areas for which measures already exist. In the UK, the *Every Child Matters* outcome target for 'Be Healthy' is reduced to a series of 11 key indicators of which four relate to childhood obesity measures at varying ages (DCSF, 2008a). These are useful, but can also been seen as somewhat blunt tools to identify the wide range of possible aspects of support for child health. To make sense of such directives we should stop and refine our understanding, before moving headlong into implementing the directed 'measures' and 'actions' to support positive responses to these child health indicators. Perhaps, on making an assessment of our local community, there are other ways to support healthy children, appropriate to locally identified needs and contexts.

Point for reflection

Based on your own knowledge of your own practice consider these key questions:

- What does 'Be Healthy' mean to you?
- What does 'A Healthy Child' actually look like, and act like?
- What pictures are conjured up in your mind when you think of a healthy child?
- What does it mean to support 'The highest attainable standard of health' for children (UNICEF, 1990: 8)?

What do we mean by 'a healthy child?'

As reflective practitioners, we need to be aware of the way an understanding of the terms 'Health' and 'Healthy Child' are social constructs. That is, they are determined by a collective social understanding at a certain point in time. This can be further explained if we reflect on images of children throughout history. There are changing concepts of a healthy child according to changing social contexts. Think of the 'rosy-cheeked plump cherub' portrayed in Victorian paintings (who would probably be considered overweight and perhaps inactive today). At the time, absence of poverty and starvation was an indicator of health (and plumpness was an indicator of wealth). Now compare that image with the later 1930s' vision of the lithe, physically strong, but lean child often pictured at the seashore, or enjoying the open air of the countryside. The air outside was cleaner as a result of environmental measures and there was more scientific awareness of the value of daylight, fresh air and physical activity. Socially people were 'buying in' to the concept of healthy active lifestyles and feeling the benefits of this.

Today there are social perspectives that present us with images of both obesity in children, and 'size zero' teenage models. The media can easily report how children have been undernourished despite parents' best intentions as they have been provided with healthy wholemeal cereals and skimmed milk giving insufficient nourishment for the child's needs. However, in contrast, many other reports provide a picture of the obese child raised on junk food. There are also black and white pictures of sunken-eyed sadness presenting charity advertisements supporting child mental health issues. Cooper et al. (2005: xi) tell us that one in ten children today in the UK are likely to suffer from some form of mental health problem. This contrasting information makes it difficult for us to visualise a current collective concept of a healthy child. Is childhood really in crisis? Are we perhaps too often presented with a mixture of 'cared for' children in clean, sweetly scented clothes (as in washing powder advertisements) in direct contrast to children in a soap opera portrayed as unable to cope with the pressures they face in today's society? In which case, what might be the response from several practitioners when asked to consider their image of a healthy child?

A picture of practice: images of a healthy child

Practitioners were asked the question, 'What is a healthy child?' At first, they found the answer difficult, however after a short time they suggested these 'emerging ideas':

> I suppose we don't really step back and think that much like this ... I, we ... picture a healthy child as active, physically and mentally, who is cared for, who is running around, happy, smiling, talking with other children, full of energy and 'pzang'! (Nicki Ovel and Linda Picken – Children's Centre Childcare Managers, Merry-Go-Round Nursery, Hereford)

> What constitutes a healthy child? ... It is easy to assume that this question is aimed at diet, quality foods and growth, and partly it is. When looking at a child, what they consume is important, but it is only a small area to be considered ... Just because the child has a good diet does not qualify the child as healthy. Good physical health has to be balanced with good mental health. One cannot exist totally without the other; as the saying goes we need 'a healthy mind and body'. (Steve Cooper, Nursery Manager)

> I see that children can have impairments, be disabled, but still be healthy in mind and spirit, still have that energy and enjoyment for life, being healthy is much more than being physically able, it's about the way you think about yourself. (Tony Andrews, Play Development Coordinator)

Physical, or social and emotional well-being indicators?

It is usual for settings to describe 'being healthy' as something which involves physical development such as the outdoor area, opportunities for physical play, the 'healthy eating' snack time, or lunch menu. The three frank and very different emergent reflections on the definition of 'healthy' that came from the practitioners have something in common. They move beyond these physical concerns to concepts of energy, mental well-being and enjoyment as indicators of health. Laevers (2000) suggested that for positive development to occur, children need to be high on emotional well-being. Well-being for Laevers is 'the degree to which children feel at ease, act spontaneously and show vitality and self-confidence' in the setting (Laevers, 2000: 24). His indicators of 'well-being' in a child include:

- openness and receptivity;
- flexibility;
- self-confidence and self-esteem;
- assertiveness;
- vitality;
- relaxation and inner peace;
- enjoyment;
- feeling 'in touch' and connected with him/herself (Laevers, 2000).

Perhaps we could use Laevers' indicators to reveal the health of children in our services and settings? By doing so, we might consider the work of Underdown (2006) who argues that finding effective ways to promote children's well-being might be key to significant improvements in all-round health.

Point for reflection

How is the well-being of children in your setting?

Do you set aside time to observe children to consider this aspect of their healthy development?

Medical, social models, and more

Our consideration of what it means to be healthy earlier in this chapter moves us to consider how perceptions of childhood and child health have changed throughout history. Social constructs of healthiness have changed according to perceived social, economic, nutrition and health priorities; as these priorities are addressed so new ones emerge to take their place. In the past there was a fear of 'plagues' or contagious infections, the priority was to ensure that the contagion was limited (though hygiene measures and vaccinations). A healthy child would have been one that was sufficiently well nourished and able to withstand a bout of infection. Health was therefore absence from disease. Workers from the 18th century began to be at the receiving end of measures to improve their health and therefore maintain productivity, and this began to determine a link between health and economic well-being. Children were also a part of the workforce, perhaps accompanying their parents to work. Responsibility for child ill-health was later often placed behind closed doors, within the family 'unit', and specifically with the mother (Webster and French, 2002). Moving forward to the post-Second World War period, we see improvements in medical research and understanding. This period was one of experts who would practise broad surveillance (including regular checks on child health), identify health deficits and implement ways of dealing with these deficits. Webster and French argue that this second stage of public health (in the first part of the 20th century) was 'dominated by health education in schools' and 'was underpinned by a victim blaming philosophy' (Webster and French, 2002: 7). This approach of reactive 'intervention' to solve identified health deficits is often termed the 'Medical Model' of health (Gradwell, 2002). In this model there is a perception that the disabled or sick child has something 'wrong' with them which prevents them from carrying out the 'normal' range of activities. The model assumes that we need to 'cure' the impairment or sickness or manage it to enable the child to fully participate in society. This model of deficit is one that has perhaps been experienced by the current generation of childcare workers.

The resilience of concepts of scientific truths in exacting 'development norms' and age-related 'milestones' are based on such medical models. Many practitioners believe that if a child has not achieved X stage at Y age, we could be concerned something must be wrong and identify an intervention plan. However, child X may not be walking at 14 months because of the specific context that surrounds his or her development, including interaction with the environment. Care must be taken to step back and consider the development of the whole child, and the impact on the child when any 'intervention' is decided upon. It is also important to acknowledge the child's rights and involvement in the decision-making processes rather than rely heavily on leading experts' perceptions. By doing so, we begin to move towards a 'Social Model' of health which implies a collective responsibility for 'health' and 'healthy children'. 'Health' is shaped by a social and cultural context. It is a condition representing more than the mere absence of illness or disease, or 'developmental delay' and is in line with the World Health Organisation's definition of 1946 in which health is defined as 'a state of complete physical, mental and social well-being' (WHO, 1946: i). Children with or without impairments can be included in the general activity because society is arranged differently to accept difference and diversity. Whilst recognising the influence and responsibilities of society for a healthy nation, such a model also seeks to 'empower' individuals to take control of their health, and make decisions about solutions. This perspective aligns with the concept of 'Rights' for children and Article 17 of the UN Rights of the child affirms that:

> State Parties shall ensure that the child has access to information and material from a diversity of national and international sources, especially those aimed at the promotion of his or her social, spiritual and moral well-being and physical and mental health. (UNICEF, 1990: 6)

Positive health, and information to support this, is a child's 'right'. Practitioners who subscribe to such a perspective will take time to understand the social context of the child and listen to the child's expressed views and opinions. They will work collaboratively and proactively with colleagues, parents, and children, and strive for the best solution to any issues arising.

Point for reflection

You should perhaps reflect upon and adopt a healthy criticism of both models. You need to take time to look at health from different perspectives. You should also draw on the 'lenses' of the parents, the child and the other professionals. It is important to return to a personal concept of health and what experiences led you to a view of that concept. This may help to best support the particular children with whom you have greatest contact. There is also likely to be greater consistency of experience for the children you work with.

It is also important to recognise the different cultural and religious differences that exist within society today. These have an influence on attitudes and the way practitioners respond to diversity within their community. Albon and Mukherji (2008) devote a chapter to this aspect in their book and underpin the fact that we should not ignore the symbolic importance of food and culture in forming the identities of individuals. We should also celebrate the positive way some settings are underpinning their policies and practice with an emphasis on health and well-being. For example, one setting wove an interpretation of their own values into an acronym for staff training and ongoing practice: it also underpins their philosophy about promoting children's health.

> Good physical health has to be balanced with good mental health. One cannot exist totally without the other. The mind and body are very complex and we understand small early problems can lead to larger future repercussions. We wanted our practitioners to be aware of the need to support both mind and body, and as a result the need arose to create an acronym to help them understand and remember our holistic philosophy. This is our holistic concept of a healthy child and the foundation philosophy of our healthy practice.
>
> **C.H.I.L.D.**
>
> **C is for confidence, self-esteem, self-reliance and self-worth**. Early years education and care must be aimed at achieving this, through well thought-out environments and a balance of child-and adult-initiated activities that incorporate the child's interests.
>
> **H is for a healthy diet**. The promotion of healthy eating is important. Educating children and also parents is paramount in our role of care. Promoting the thinking of healthy eating can be done every day at snack and lunch times, and also in the home corner during free play.
>
> **I is for imagination.** This should be at the centre of every child, as it is in this acronym. A child without imagination is a child lost. Children's imagination is crucial for development and emotional health. Expression allows children to vent anxieties and feelings through their creations and play.
>
> **L is for love attachments**. Children need love and an understanding that exist outside the family unit. A child who knows and feels that they are loved and wanted has the foundations of good emotional health and stability.
>
> **D is for developmental nutrition** and experiences that promote thinking. Different experiences enhance brain development through synaptic promotion. Oxygen is the ultimate brain food; outside play must be considered to be a major part of the child's day. When looking at environments, none lend themselves to imagination and stimulation better than an outside natural experience. (Steve Cooper, Nursery Manager)

Summary

As an early years practitioner, you are living in a time of easily accessed information. There is new health evidence emerging daily. Much of what you are presented with may well contrast with previous information. We also know that children's health needs are likely to be individual and related to contextual experiences. It is imperative that practitioners are reflective and able to look critically at information and adapt their practice accordingly. This is valuable because governments also have particular perspectives on issues and key health priorities that may

(Continued)

(Continued)

seem to be constantly changing. An instant reaction to a new piece of information, or policy awareness, is often to consider the statistics, or social benefit or policy statements as definitive and persuasive. You are then asked to take on that information and dutifully agree to implement policy. Trying to follow 'by the letter' given policies on health can lead to one template and a standardisation of services 'imposed' on settings and children. Charles Handy writes of the need for us all to be 'leaders in our own sphere', not 'cogs in somebody else's wheel hurtling God knows where' (Handy, 2004: 4). The words of policy documents are often open to interpretation. A reflective practitioner will understand that there are different ways of doing things, will question what is presented and provide a response based on their own interpretation. A reflective practitioner will also be prepared to work with others. Friedman argues that in order to reach key societal goals or outcomes, we need to have a common vision and common language, we need to decide where we are going, and what it will look like when we get there, and stick to it. Changing goals according to latest policy research, often targeted at different service sectors, will not necessarily enable us to meet longer-term health outcomes (Friedman, 2005). In order to travel in the right direction, we need to have common, agreed measures of success towards the given vision and be consistent in supporting these (UNICEF, 2007). A child will not be healthy just because a healthy eating programme has been implemented as part of Government policy. Neither will he or she necessarily be healthy because a deficit in development has been identified and an action plan put in place. Supporting child health is a long-term aim, which draws on social constructivist ideals, and recognises diversity.

Suggested further reading

- Albon, A. and Mukherji, P. (2008) *Food and Health in Early Childhood.* London: Sage Publications.

  This book provides an overview of food and eating in the early years, but also considers the impact of policy and culture on the health of early years children.

- Palmer, S. (2006) *Toxic Childhood: How the Modern World Is Damaging Our Children and What We Can Do About It.* London: Orion.

  This book argues for a return to more traditional values and presents a challenging perspective of how children can generate their health and well-being though play, exercise and outdoor adventure.

References

Albon, A. and Mukherji, P. (2008) *Food and Health in Early Childhood.* London: Sage Publications.

Cooper, M., Hooper, C. and Thompson, M. (2005) *Child and Adolescent Mental Health: Theory and Practice*. London: Hodder Arnold.

Department for Children, Schools and Families (DCSF) (2007) 'The Children's Plan fact sheet: children and young people's health'. http://www.dcsf.gov.uk/childrensplan/facts-health.shtml (accessed 19.01.2009).

Department for Children, Schools and Families (DCSF) (2008a) 'Every Child Matters Outcomes Framework'. http://publications.everychildmatters.gov.uk/eOrderingDownload/DCSF-00331-2008.pdf (accessed 21.01.2009).

Department for Children, Schools and Families (DCSF) (2008b) 'Every Child Matters: outcomes for children and young people'. http://www.everychildmatters.gov.uk/aims/outcomes/ (accessed 15.01.2009).

Department for Children, Schools and Families (DCSF) (2008c) *Practice Guidance for the Early Years Foundation Stage*. Nottingham: DCSF.

Department of Health (DoH) (2004) *The National Service Framework for Children, Young People and Maternity Services*. London: HMSO.

Friedman, M. (2005) *Trying Hard Is Not Good Enough*. New York: Trafford.

Gradwell, L. (2002) 'Disability and public health', in L. Adams, M. Amos and J. Munro (eds), *Promoting Health: Policies and Practice*. London: Sage Publications.

Handy, C. (2004) *The Empty Raincoat*. London: Arrow.

Laevers, F. (2000) 'Forward to basics! Deep level learning and the experiential approach', *Early Years*, 20(2): 20–8.

Lajole, J. and Leveille, S. (2007) *The Well Being of Children in Wealthy Countries; UNICEF Report Card 7 – CECW Information Sheet No. 52E*. Montreal, QC: McGill University School of Social Work.

Maslow, A. (1943) 'A theory of human motivation', *Psychological Review*, 50(4): 370–96.

Palmer, S. (2006) *Toxic Childhood: How the Modern World is Damaging Our Children and What We Can Do About It*. London: Orion.

Shribman, S. (2007) *Children's Health, Our Future: A Review of Progress against the National Service Framework for Children, Young People and Maternity Services 2004*. London: Department of Health.

Underdown, A. (2006) *Health and Well Being in Early Childhood*. London: McGraw-Hill.

United Nations Children's Fund (UNICEF) (1990) *The United Nations Convention on the Rights of the Child: Adopted and Opened for Signature, Ratification and Accession by General Assembly Resolution 44/25 of 20 November 1989*. London: UNICEF UK.

United Nations Children's Fund (UNICEF) (2007) *Child Poverty in Perspective: An Overview of Child Well-Being in Rich Countries, Innocenti Report Card 7*. Florence: UNICEF Innocenti Research Centre.

Webster, C. and French, J. (2002) 'The cycle of conflict: the history of the public health and health promotion movements', in L. Adams, M. Amos and J. Munro (eds), *Promoting Health: Policies and Practice*. London: Sage Publications.

World Health Organisation (WHO) (1946) *Preamble to the Constitution as Adopted by the International Health Conference, New York, 19–22 June 1946*. New York: WHO.

Section 3

Enabling Professional Environments

7

Children's Centres and Children's Services?

Michael Reed

Chapter objectives

The chapter explores Sure Start children's centres (SSCC) and considers:

- the driving forces that have promoted the development of SSCCs in England;
- the services available at a centre and the benefits to children and families;
- a picture of practice looking at some of the roles and responsibilities of those involved in leading and managing a centre.

Driving forces

Over the past decade, early years care and education has been significantly driven forward by Government initiatives. Change has been fuelled by a raft of policies and strategies introduced with the aim of supporting the welfare of children and families. The way childcare is financed has been radically overhauled and legislation put in place that has enshrined in law the educational expectations of parents. The way early years practitioners are trained has changed as have the qualifications available. Practitioners are expected to engage with parents, share information with other agencies and engage in partnership working. Today, all professionals are trained to realise they have a responsibility for safeguarding children's well-being. They are trained to realise the importance of the learning environment, and the educational value of observation, assessment, and planning. Essentially, there is a developing consensus throughout the UK about the roles and responsibilities of those involved in supporting young children and their families. Such changes have not been enacted without considerable debate. This has focused on new professional roles, the value of reflective practice and the importance of professional development as well as changes in management and leadership (Aubrey, 2007; Murray, 2009; Nurse, 2007; Owen and Haynes 2008; Pound, 2008; Reed, 2008).

A useful starting point to consider the way these developments have been forged was the publication of *Every Child Matters* in 2003 (DfES, 2003). This was paralleled in Scotland with 'Getting it right for every child: proposals for action' (Scottish Government, 2005). These reports highlighted the need for common goals to help and support families, which now underpin policy and practice in England and influenced developments in the remainder of the UK. The goals focus upon:

- protecting vulnerable children;
- providing opportunities for children to enjoy and achieve;
- allowing children to make a positive contribution;
- providing opportunities for children and families to achieve economic well-being.

In addition, there has been a nationwide call to develop shared values between different professions and to engage in shared training. It is now seen as essential that professionals work together and share common goals to provide 'joined-up' working considering the 'whole child' and the child within the family. These are reflected in the skills contained in the *Common Core of Skills and Knowledge* (DfES, 2005). These are required by those (including volunteers) whose work brings them into regular contact with children, young people and families. The 'core skills and knowledge' underline the need for professionals to work together and therefore be more effective in supporting the interests of the child. They are described under six main headings and ask practitioners to demonstrate:

- effective communication and engagement with children, young people and families;
- child and young person development;
- safeguarding and promoting the welfare of the child;
- supporting transitions;
- multi-agency working;
- sharing information.

The Children's Workforce Network (2009) has built upon the requirements of the 'Core' and produced a Functional Map that gives further direction on aspects of leadership and inclusion. Both documents are important and are embedded in the CWDC Sector-Endorsed Foundation Degree (2008b). This is a qualification for experienced practitioners with an appropriate level 3 qualification who are employed in the children's workforce. They are skills that may be refined and developed as circumstances and developments dictate, but the idea of a 'common core' of skills and knowledge for all practitioners will become an essential component of childcare strategy in the future. The strategy will draw upon the views of an 'expert group' drawn from the Children's Workforce Network, the Schools Workforce Social Partnership, the NHS and other services. The group will engage with the Government to propose ways of developing professional skills of the early years workforce and consider contemporary developments such as the award of Early Years Professional Status (EYPS). The intention is to have in place a graduate EYP in every full day-care setting by 2015 (CWDC, 2008a).

Legislative changes have also been necessary to support change. In England, the Childcare Act 2006 reinforced parents' expectations for the provision of high-quality childcare services and confirmed the role of local education authorities as leaders in forging partnerships across all sectors. This is also recognised within the Children's Plan in 2007 and changes to the 'early years curriculum' in England and the introduction of the Early Years Foundation Stage (EYFS) (DCSF, 2008). Indeed, this curriculum is now reinforced with a statutory framework, which requires adherence to a variety of initiatives to support children and their families. Practitioners are asked to consider the 'whole child', ensuring that they work with professionals from other agencies and share information between different settings a child may attend. This approach is underpinned in the Common Assessment Framework (CAF) (DfES, 2006). The framework brings together a common form of assessment that can be utilised within a number of early years settings, such as children's centres, schools, early years facilities, health services, and the voluntary sector. It starts with the unborn child and follows them into adolescence. It promotes changes to the way professionals perceive roles and responsibilities, and considers the need for a 'lead professional' to coordinate services. There have also been changes in Scotland, Wales, and Northern Ireland. They too reinforce the need for change and actions, and underline the importance of integrated working, safeguarding children's welfare, longitudinal assessment, specialised early years teaching, and the need for a defined curriculum framework. There is also a desire to enhance the status of the workforce and promote professional development and see trained early years professionals as an important component of change. This can be seen in Northern Ireland, where there is a wide variety of qualifications within the early years and the school sector (Walsh, 2007). Nursery schools and classes have a qualified teacher, and the private and voluntary sector are required to have support from a qualified teacher or an early years specialist.

In the future, the Northern Ireland Social Care Council (NISCC) will monitor and inform developments and draw together agencies to implement change. In Wales the aim of the Welsh Assembly Government is to provide part-time nursery places for all 3-year-olds in Wales, and to develop integrated centres offering wrap-around childcare and education. From 2008, a foundation stage for 3- to 7-year-olds has been introduced. There is now a clear strategy, which aims to improve the skills of the children's workforce and provide career progression (Children and Young People's Workforce Development Network Wales, 2005). For Scotland in 2007 the Scottish Social Services Council (SSSC) produced a report that required a movement towards a more fully trained workforce advocating a national performance and qualifications framework (QAA Scotland, 2007). This has been taken forward by the Scottish Government and the Convention of Scottish Local Authorities (COSLA) who produced a report which describes early years and early intervention support (Scottish Government, 2008). It gives a context for a national performance framework, and proposes a list of tasks to be taken forward as part of the framework.

Point for reflection

It can be argued that the UK is moving towards a common consensus about the services a child and their family should receive. There is also a developing consensus about a professional expectation for those who act as early years practitioners. Moreover, that professional qualifications and training are seen as essential in raising standards and promoting ways for professionals to work together. The cumulative effect of a decade of 'driving forces' has certainly moved early years care and education towards the top of the education agenda. We wait to see if this will be sustained and welcome any attempt to measure the impact of such developments on the care and education of children.

Sure Start children's centres

It can be argued that the development of Sure Start children's centres embodies the consensus that is forming around ways to support children and families. In England they are a means of drawing together education, care, family support, a range of health services and practical help for those seeking employment. They were also intended to be a place where the expertise of the workforce could be developed and also serve communities in rural areas as well as those in towns and cities (Sure Start, date unknown). They are established as part of a 'community hub', initially, to serve the needs of those in areas of social deprivation, more recently to support comunities in all areas of the country. In terms of services they are located in buildings – some purpose built, others adapted from existing childcare centres – but all offering access and advice for parents to locate good quality early learning combined with full day-care provision for children. Inclusive practice is also a high priority which encompases support for children with special needs and their parents. This is further combined with good quality teacher input and an emphasis upon early learning and child and family health services, including antenatal services, and a mechanism to support parents in their home. Children's centres are also intended to be a focal point for developing facilities that rest upon extending and developing existing expertise, for example developing a local childminder network. Local authorities have responsibility for their development in consultation with parents, the private, voluntary and independent sector.

Between 2004 and 2008 the intention was to spend £3.2 billion on children's centres and Sure Start local programmes, but centres may also derive their income from various other sources including grants and fees for childcare charged to parents. Early signs were that more needs to be done to reach and support some of the most excluded groups and that the cost of running centres was varied (NAO, 2006). There are now nearly 2,900 centres open, with almost 2 million families engaged in the range of services on offer. The government is committed to having 3,500 children's centres throughout England by 2010, one for every community, so that every child and family can benefit from the services on offer (Sure Start, date unknown). Some children's centres may have a sessional nursery or day-care centre. Others may provide diverse services such as a link with a Citizens Advice Bureau, a 'young parents group' or 'baby massage'. However, a common thread that runs between them is an ethos, which attempts to reduce professional barriers, and sees professional expertise as something that collectively works for the benefit of parents and children. Such an approach also encompasses a desire to see the range of services as complementary rather than in competition with each other.

Point for reflection

It is worth considering what an integrated centre can actually offer parents. If they are no more than an 'educational shopping mall' then they may not be delivering what they have promised. Instead, they should be seen as providing longer-term help and support, especially to those parents on the margins of communities. The following small 'pictures of practice' may explain their immediate and longer-term impact.

A picture of practice – engaging with children's centres

Mary is in her late twenties bringing up her young child and living in 'supported accommodation' provided by a registered charity. Her accommodation is in close proximity to a local children's centre and she was actively encouraged to make use of the Centre and its resources. When she

(Continued)

(Continued)

first became involved with the Centre, she was relying on alcohol to relieve the stress of a failed (and abusive) personal relationship. She engages in regular meetings with other parents to gain support, practical advice and develop her own skills as a 'parent with prospects'. This has required hard work and developing a partnership of trust with those professionals at the centre who have supported her over some years. She has now built on previous qualifications and gained Mathematics and English GCSEs. She is now in part-time employment, and intends to maintain her studies in order to register at university.

Diane is aged 16 and again lives in 'supported accommodation' near to the children's centre. She joined a 'young mothers' group' because she needed support to develop her parenting skills. She and her partner have attended family support sessions at the centre and found the support from a community worker has allowed them to develop and refine their skills as parents. This has led to Diane working on a voluntary basis at the nursery attached to the centre and developing expertise in working with young children. She is currently completing a National Vocational Qualification in Childcare and Education. The centre also provided support for her partner. This was done by providing practical guidance to gain employment and he is now in full-time work.

Linda has taken advantage of extended day-care for her young child. She did this in order to return to employment. She needed help and advice to do this, which included developing her literacy skills and building her confidence to engage fully with others and recognise that she did have skills, which an employer would welcome. The centre was supportive in allowing her to find employment that was 'family friendly' and she is now employed part-time at a local firm.

Brian is a single parent and he too needed help to gain employment in order that he could generate an income and support his young son. He attended a support group at the centre aimed at 'fathers'. He is now is much involved in maintaining and developing the 'fathers' group' and hopes he can use his own experience to help others. He too has taken advantage of childcare options and welcomed the advice from a variety of agencies to help him support his family. It is interesting that he does not see his experience as a one-way process, with him becoming dependant upon services. Instead he perceives the centre as a location where a number of services came together which meant less time spent explaining the same things to different people, less bureaucracy and services that speak (as he put it) the same language.

These 'pictures' are by no means untypical of the support provided at a Sure Start children's centre. Indeed, the emphasis on helping people to gain employment and enhance their economic independence is paramount in all centres (Sure Start, 2008). Family support is also a key factor in all centres. This consists of services such as home visiting, parenting programmes, relationship support, adult education and family learning, and employment training (Apps et al., 2007)

A range of services

Children's centres provide a range of coordinated services. These can be established by those working directly at a centre or in tandem with other providers such as those from the health service and more recently extended schools. Let us try to illustrate the services on offer from one centre, remembering that there is no such thing as a 'typical children's centre'.

Figure 7.1 illustrates the range of services and resources available in a children's centre. It is not intended to reveal which professional coordinates which service. This is because it is important to have a view of integrated working where professionals collaborate and develop their own skills, but actively engage in shared professional experience with others (Reed, 2009). We should also remember the important role of administrative and support staff, including those who maintain the buildings and those from the local authority who assist in coordination and forward planning alongside those managing the centre. There are also links with other agencies such as local schools, pre-schools, and training establishments. Some of the services at a centre may also be 'commissioned' or brought into a centre as needed. Others have evolved and emerged as a response to community needs. However, just presenting a list of services or describing a range of provision is not sufficient to convey the complexity of what a centre does. Care needs to be taken in how these services are offered. A recent report from Ofsted (2008) indicated the importance of a well-coordinated service. The report suggested that where coordination was good, take-up had improved. This underlines the importance of leadership and the value of well-coordinated interagency working as an important factor for success. It is also worth noting that the quality of local authorities' strategic leadership is also seen as important, especially when they are directly involved in the development and monitoring of services (Ofsted, 2008).

Point for reflection

It is important to see children's centres as 'communities' facilitating a range of services. Voluntary sector groups may develop some services as will parents who use the centre. It would be all too easy to see a children's centre as a place where there is a co-location of services rather than integrating services and encouraging professional

(Continued)

Access to: Local Authority Officers
Safeguarding Children processes

Staff training for professional qualifications
Sharing specialist aspects of professional development

Childminding support and Childminding Network

Smoking Cessation Group – Enuresis Advice

Home Start
Family Support Services
Play Worker Services

Infant Toddler Group
Crèche
'WrapAround' school links
Fun 2 Talk Group

Developmental assessment/checks
Baby Clinic
Ante- and Post-Natal Support
Breastfeeding/weaning Group

Healthy eating programme linked to the nursery and childminding network

Oral Health meetings
Health Visitor 'drop in' sessions

Nursery and day-care centre
Forest Schools Project

Support for vulnerable families

Craft group for parents

Baby Massage Group
Baby Sign and Rhyme

Children and families

Speech/language support
Access to health and well-being services
Common Assessment Framework

Fathers' Group

Stay and Play Group

Carer and Toddler Group

Saturday support group (sensory impairment)

Keep Fit/Healthy Living
Nutritionist advice
Jump Start Play Sessions

Informal coffee mornings

Young Parents To-Be Group

Outreach home visiting

Early Intervention for children with special educational needs and Portage programme

Private Providers Network

Rooms for community use and access to community Toy Library

Access/links to social workers. Inclusion officer. Educational Psychologist. Family Support Service Portage Team. GPs

Figure 7.1 An illustration of the range of services at a children's centre

(Continued)

partnerships. It is therefore important to see a children's centre as moving away from just the 'provision' of services towards developing a community of practice where children, families and early childhood professionals actively engage with each other. It is also important to see the centre as not overwhelming local services and this requires a delicate balance between support and intrusion.

Leadership

Those leading and managing an integrated setting need to have a realistic and perceptive view of inter-professional working. It requires them to have knowledge of the career histories, roles, and responsibilities of all professionals at a centre. A centre may house:

- Health Visitors with responsibility for coordinating developmental assessment and providing support for parents;
- Early Years Professionals who offer advice on education and care and coordinate curriculum development and assessment;
- Community Support Workers who coordinates services to families;
- Volunteers who help to resource, plan, maintain and develop such things as an early years resource centre or a toy library;
- Teachers who develops partnerships with local schools.

They will all have a role in shaping the educational philosophy of the centre. There may also be specialist Portage Workers, who support children with special educational needs and staff who coordinate work with parents to support a healthy lifestyle or deal with social problems experienced by families. Coordinating such a range of professionals requires a leader to encourage everyone to share knowledge and expertise. Doing so may bring more focused attention on the child and his or her family and less replication between different professionals. Working together means there is likely to be a shared understanding of practice and less time spent overcoming professional barriers. This is because there will inevitably arise occasional disputes over professional boundaries, ideological issues and approaches to meeting the needs of individual parents. A leader must strive to foster a genuine desire to change working practices, shed preconceived ideas, and have a clear view of different professional roles. What is more, leading a centre requires considerable skills of time management and the ability to enact change in a measured and purposeful way. Of course establishing such a shared vision takes time and the leader and his or her co-workers will have to give their professional commitment freely in order to make the service work. The leader also needs to be adept at managing budgets and prioritising which service should be extended, developed, or refined. Inevitably, this means there is a continual need to prioritise resources and to promote a culture of innovation and continuing professional development.

The role can be described as being multi-faceted and is likely to extend well beyond the physical area of the centre into the community. It also includes developing robust evaluation programmes in order to ascertain the impact on the lives of parents and children. Added to this is the production of regular financial reports for a Management Committee and ensuring that the work of the centre complies with legislative and regulatory requirements. A further challenge is establishing performance management structures for a disparate professional workforce. To all these demands can be added a clear understanding of the way external inspection services operate.

Point for reflection

The development of Sure Start children's centres has been driven by Government initiatives and finance. This has involved developing new ways of working and the emergence of 'early years leaders' who are now at the forefront of change. They are what Aubrey (2007) sees as being engaged in flexible leadership to support different models of multi-agency working. This requires practitioners who are not always part of such developments to understand why such change is necessary and for those most closely involved to become engaged in reviewing their own practice. The key challenge for the delivery of effective family support is to find and engage the families who stand to gain most from effective family support, while managing catchment, operational and funding changes. (Apps et al., 2007)

Such demands require a questioning and reflective approach to understanding change and one's attitude to change (Simkins, 2007). Simkins suggests considering the process through which we learn about new and established developments, and start to theorise about our work and place it within a wider social, cultural and political context. This allows for a consideration of values and principles upon which practice is based and to challenge unquestioned assumptions. There is little doubt, integrated centres are starting to play a significant and pivotal role in the delivery of children's services. Therefore, practitioners need to be keenly aware of the changes in policy and practice that are taking place. They need to know why these are happening and what underpinning framework and philosophy drives them forward. It is difficult to argue with the premise that local communities, children, and parents should be supported to maximise their potential. However, it is possible to consider if centres are imposed upon communities, or are evolving from community needs. It is also possible to question the speed of change and the demands placed upon leaders and practitioners in enacting such change. Reflection also means we should learn from 'best practice'. This is more than imitation; it is how to assimilate knowledge that is embedded in the work of successful practitioners.

Summary

There is little doubt that centres are becoming a vehicle for refining and adjusting existing roles and professional relationships. They now serve 2 million children and their families. The National Evaluation of Sure Start (Sure Start, 2008) found that children behave better if they live in areas with SSCCs. Other findings showed that parents have more positive parenting skills, thus helping prepare children to do well at school. The Government wants to ensure that centres are now enshrined in law, because centres have no defined identity in law. They are currently just one way in which local authorities and their partners can choose to provide integrated early childhood services to meet their duties under the Childcare Act 2006. It is now proposed to make centres a legally recognised part of the universal infrastructure for children's services. Importantly, the proposals suggest that regular consultation with parents and the wider community should take place on how they feel about current provision and developing future services. This will go some way to consider how practice may be refined, improved, or changed.

There are still key questions to address:

- Should the personal qualities which underpin interagency working be explored in more detail as Wendy Messenger considers in her chapter?
- Does co-locating services in one place really mean that the services themselves are somehow integrated?
- Does having a large interagency establishment in the community mean that one aspect of service provision is given a higher profile than others?
- What place has the voluntary sector within a system that has children's centres acting as a hub for early years services?

There are no immediate answers to these questions. However, we do know that integrated children's centres are here to stay. They are changing

(Continued)

(Continued)

the landscape of early years provision. Practitioners based in centres are increasingly reflecting on how best to support children and families and starting to enquire into their own actions and share aspects of good practice. This chapter has only produced a 'snapshot' of change. Time will tell if the resources needed to sustain services and therefore maximise the impact of children's centres will be maintained.

Suggested further reading

- Canning, N. (2009) 'Empowering communities through inspirational leadership', in A. Robins and S. Callan (eds), *Managing Early Years Settings*. London: Sage Publications.
  This chapter considers the importance of recognising the value of individual contributions within an early years setting and how they are woven together to support the development and sustainability of a setting.

- Western, S. (2007) *Leadership: A Critical Text*. London: Sage Publications.
  This book provides a critical overview of leadership and examines the micro and macro aspects of policy.

- Wright, J., Stackhouse, J. and Wood, J. (2008) 'Promoting language and literacy skills in the early years: lessons from interdisciplinary teaching and learning', *Child Language Teaching and Therapy*, 24(2): 155–71.
  This article considers the importance of interprofessional working and how this is achieved through the context of promoting language and literacy skills.

References

Apps, J., Reynolds, J., Ashby, V. and Husain, F. (2007) *Family Support in Children's Centres: Planning, Commissioning and Delivery*. London: Family and Parenting Institute.

Aubrey, C. (2007) *Leading and Managing in the Early Years*. London: Sage Publications.

Children and Young People's Workforce Development Network Wales (2005) 'Children's and Young People's Workforce Strategy for Wales'. http://www.ccwales.org.uk/DesktopDefault.aspx?tabid=606 (accessed 10.12.2008).

Children's Workforce Development Council (CWDC) (2008a) 'Early Years Professional Status'. http://www.cwdcouncil.org.uk/eyps (accessed 09.01.2009).

Children's Workforce Development Council (CWDC) (2008b) 'Sector-endorsed foundation degree: criteria for the new model'. http://www.cwdcouncil.org.uk/foundation-degrees/sector-endorsement/ey-se-criteria (accessed 09.01.2009).

Children's Workforce Network (2009) *Functional Map of the Children's and Young People's Workforce in England*. Leeds: Children's Workforce and Development Council (CWDC). www.cwdcouncil.org.uk

Department for Children, Schools and Families (DCSF) (2007) *The Children's Plan: Building Brighter Futures*. London: HMSO.

Department for Children, Schools and Families (DCSF) (2008) *Practice Guidance for the Early Years Foundation Stage*. Nottingham: DCFS.

Department for Education and Skills (DfES) (2003) *Every Child Matters: Change for Children*. Nottingham: DfES.

Department for Education and Skills (DfES) (2005) *Common Core of Skills and Knowledge for the Children's Workforce*. Nottingham: DfES.

Department for Education and Skills (DfES) (2006) 'Common Assessment Framework for children and young people'. http://www.everychildmatters.gov.uk/deliveringservices/caf/ (accessed 09.01.2009).

Murray, J. (2009) 'Value based leadership and management', in A. Robins and S. Callan (eds), *Managing Early Years Settings*. London: Sage Publications.

National Audit Office (NAO) (2006) *Sure Start Children's Centres: Report by the Controller and Auditor General*. London: NAO/HMSO.

Northern Ireland Social Care Council (NISCC) (date unknown) 'Introduction'. http://www.niscc.info/intro.htm (accessed 13.12.2008).

Nurse, A. (ed.) (2007) *The New Early Years Professional: Dilemmas and Debates*. London: David Fulton.

Office for Standards in Education (Ofsted) (2008) *The Impact of Children's Centres and Extended Schools*. Ref No.: NR- 2008–02. London: HMSO.

Owen, S. and Haynes, G. (2008) 'Developing professionalism in the early years: from policy to practice', in L. Miller and C. Cable (eds), *Professionalism in the Early Years*. London: Hodder Education.

Pound, L. (2008) 'Exploring leadership: roles and responsibilities of the early years professional', in A. Paige-Smith and A. Craft (eds), *Developing Reflective Practice in the Early Years*. Maidenhead: Open University Press.

Quality Assurance Agency (QAA) Scotland (2007) 'The standard for childhood practice'. http://www.qaa.ac.uk/academicinfrastructure/benchmark/scottish/earlyYears.asp (accessed 10.12.2008).

Reed, M. (2008) 'Professional development through reflective practice', in A. Paige-Smith and A. Craft (eds), *Developing Reflective Practice in the Early Years*. Maidenhead: Open University Press.

Reed, M. (2009) 'Partnership working in the early years', in A. Robins and S. Callan (eds), *Managing Early Years Settings*. London: Sage Publications.

Scottish Government (2005) 'Getting it right for every child: proposals for action'. www.scotland.gov.uk/Publications/2005/06/20135608/56173 (accessed 09.01.2009).

Scottish Government (2008) 'Early years and early intervention: a joint Scottish Government and COSLA policy statement'. http://www.scotland.gov.uk/Publications/2008/03/14121428/6 (accessed 09.01.2009).

Simkins, T. (2007) 'Leadership in education: "what works" or "what makes sense"?', *Educational Management Administration and Leadership*, 33(1): 9–26.

Sure Start (date unknown) 'Sure Start Children's Centres Practice Guidance'. http://www.surestart.gov.uk/publications/index.cfm?document=1500 (accessed 22.01.2009).

Sure Start (2008) 'National evaluation of Sure Start research team: the impact of Sure Start Local Programmes on three years olds and their families'. http://www.surestart.gov.uk/publications/?Document=1974 (accessed 22.01.2009).

Walsh, G. (2007) 'Northern Ireland', in M.M. Clark and T. Waller (eds), *Early Childhood Education and Care: Policy and Practice*. London: Sage Publications.

8

Working Together at a Children's Centre

Rosie Walker

Chapter objectives

The chapter provides a picture of practice within one Sure Start Children's Centre (SSCC). This was done by 'listening' to the voices of those most closely involved, drawing on the expertise of parents, staff and Senior Management. It was part of my own research for a higher degree and I am deeply indebted to all those involved who gave of their time freely to assist my studies. They all played a significant part in developing my understanding of the complexity of leading and managing an SSCC. The aim was to allow reflection on models of integrated or inter-agency working within a contemporary area of early years education. It does not represent what occurs at all centres but instead suggests that it is possible to learn from and reflect upon the experiences of one setting. It draws out thoughts about future practice and exposes areas of general applicability. Importantly, it attempts to arrive at a consensus not only about what goes on at a centre but why it goes on and what this means for children and families.

As issues of integrated working begin to be untangled, the layers of complexity faced by Leaders of Centres have emerged. Government investment in early years services has been unprecedented and this has produced a raft of expectation of not only what will be delivered but also what can be achieved in terms of outcomes for children and future generations. These are purposeful and positive aims; however, they are sometimes manifested as sets of targets and an almost daily myriad of initiatives and policies. This means leaders face high levels of expectation from those who use the resources on offer, who rightly expect to receive quality.

A picture of practice – setting the context

The views emanate from a Sure Start Children's Centre, based on a primary school site, designated in April 2006. In Phase 1 (2004–06), it started (alongside many other SSCCs in England) with the aim of serving families living in the 20 per cent most disadvantaged wards (based on the Index of Multiple Deprivation) (DETR, 2000). It was an Early Years Centre in the 1980s and continued up until 2003 when Sure Start was introduced within the area. Sure Start is the Government's programme to deliver the best start in life for every child by bringing together early education, childcare, health and family support. Within the locality, it fulfilled this agenda by setting up commissioned projects, such as health and voluntary services designed to bring local professionals together to develop and extend services to provide the best start to children in their early lives. During 2006, Sure Start amalgamated with the Early Years Centre to form the Children's Centre which has continued to develop its own and commissioned services. Staffing at the centre includes the Senior Management Team (SMT) which comprises a Headteacher, from Education, a Centre Manager from a Social Work background, a Curriculum Leader and a Family Services Manager from a Nursery Nurse and Social Care background. The centre has four Community Family Workers, a Community Development Coordinator, Family Support Worker and Fieldworker. It has two Teachers, five Early Years Practitioners, three Early Years Assistants, and a Cook. Some staff work part-time. The centre is governed by a Partnership Board made up of parents and local professionals, which answers to a Children's Centre Committee of the school Governing Body.

On site is a sessional nursery facility offering places to 48 children. There is a Tiny Tots provision where vulnerable young children have sessions without parents. Healthy eating is a priority and children have a subsidised healthy lunch using vegetables they have harvested and planted themselves. There is a programme of Family Support which includes Drop-in services, Baby Groups, Stay and Play, Baby Massage, Toddler Gym as well as Outreach Home Visiting. There is Health provision through a weekly clinic and Health Visitor attendance. Commissioned projects work from the site and these include Citizen's Advice Bureau, Relate, Speech and Language support and advice, as well as Secure Start, an infant attachment

(Continued)

(Continued)

project. Within the centre, there is an extensive programme of Adult Education and Learning designed to increase confidence and improve skills and aid employment as well as build self-confidence. Within the locality, the centre has a base at a local community building where Drop-in, Music, Stress Busting, Toddler Gym sessions and a Health Clinic take place. The centre provides family support groups at a local teenage parent's housing project and commissions services to provide a befriending service, oral health promotion including dentist visits and a breastfeeding group. There are close links to local private and voluntary day-care providers.

Point for reflection

- Have you visited a Children's Centre?
- Read Chapter 7 by Michael Reed to gain additional knowledge of how SSCCs have developed and the services they provide.
- Have you talked to a parent who has been involved in a Children's Centre?
- Are you surprised by the range of services on offer?
- If you were a parent coming to the centre for the first time, how would you expect to gain access to the services on offer?

Your responses to the questions posed may echo the views of parents who attend the centre. Some have a particular view of the types of services they expect and are often amazed at the range of provision. In addition, they can be surprised at being asked to identify services that can be developed. This may be because of their life experiences and what they have previously seen in terms of a model of 'service provision'. They may be used to a medical model where they make an appointment, see a professional and receive expert advice and possibly treatment. In the main, they would expect this to be over a health issue. Some expect a 'social care model' having presented their 'problem or concern' to a professional and then receive a form of 'assessment'. Thereafter they receive some form of intervention. This may be at a time of crisis in their lives and the immediacy of the issue takes precedence over preventing the issue recurring. Alternatively, they may be used to a 'provision of education model' where their child is enrolled in a nursery and education is provided. They inspect the setting and to an extent the setting inspects them. They sometimes play a part in the selection of provision, but usually they accept the range of provision on offer. Rarely, does a setting ask them what they require. It is unsurprising that when many have come to a centre for the first time, they are a little confused as these 'models' do not fit exactly with their previous experiences. All professionals need to be aware of and consider this at length if they were asked to put themselves in the place of a 'new parent'.

The voices of parents

Parents said above all they were welcomed. This seemed a basic and rather simplistic attitudinal response, but it raises the importance of how parents perceive professional services. They indicated that their needs were discussed and recorded and suggested how this developed a 'personalised package' of services wherever possible. They felt that their views helped to inform the planning of services where existing services were not available. Parents welcomed the fact that many services were tailored around their children's needs and that many different types of service are available at the centre or in the locality. They described using the centre to build up a network of friends to relieve isolation and accessing the range of resources and activities designed for their children's learning. For example:

> I wish there were these services when my older children were little. There are so many services for children and families now. There is lots of support. (Parent of a 3-year-old at a focus group, February 2008)

> I don't think my eldest child would have been taken off me if these services were here then. (Parent of a baby at a focus group, February 2008)

> I have always been a great believer in all the professions working together under one roof. I have had to travel to different buildings and see lots of different people with my son, all of whom give different advice. When I get the professional input from one place it is much easier and less stressful. (Parent of a 6-month-old and 4-year-old, February 2008)

> This centre is a little haven: a home from home. (Parent of a 4-year-old at a focus group, March 2008)

> My daughter loves the messy play sessions, the soft play room and the Forest School best. (Parent of a 2-year-old and 4-year-old at a focus group, March 2008)

In terms of access to services, parents said how much easier it is to have Health services available as well as services such as Citizen's Advice Bureau and Relate. They provide help speedily and avert crises. It was interesting that parents easily identified the need for proactive preventative means of support – though not in these quasi-professional terms. Parents can access some services directly and some through staff who provide either targeted services or signpost or arrange for more specialised services to be brought to the centre. For example, a Child Psychotherapist worked with a family at the centre to avoid a long bus journey to an unfamiliar place. There is a mixture of specific services accessed directly and those which are filtered and require a referral process which can be speeded up through the Children's Centre. Interestingly, parents seemed not to mind which professional works with them. However, this was on many occasions qualified, by saying as long as the support and advice they received was consistent and non-conflicting. They also discussed the building up of trust between professionals and themselves making it easier to express their needs and accept more targeted services to help with parenting skills. Parents felt valued if issues were explained so they could understand and more readily accept what happens. When faced with a choice between sessions for them and sessions just for the children, they acknowledged that it was important to have as many sessions for the children as possible. In this way, they began to mirror the focus on children and meeting their needs professed by staff at the centre. For example:

> You are all so professional here in the way that you work that issues of not getting on with each other and between different professionals are not obvious to us as parents. (Parent of a 3-year-old, January 2008)

> I am very pleased with the Early Years Practitioners working with the speech therapists as my daughter gets specific help with her speech at each nursery session she attends. (Parent of a 4-year-old, March 2008)

> When I found out that the Early Years Practitioner at the centre was running the parenting course I decided to attend. I knew that I needed help with my son but I did not want anyone to know I was having problems but now I know she is running the course I feel at ease about coming along. (Parent of a baby and 3-year-old, March 2008)

> I was angry that there was not a Tiny Tots place for my daughter and asked why. The manager explained that the funding had changed and that she now had to provide 3 sessions a week for 12 two-year-olds or refuse the funding and keep to the present arrangement of 1 session a week for 24 children. I could see the dilemma she had and I told her that at a risk of not getting a place for my daughter I could see that 3 sessions a week for 12 children was better for them as one session a week for a two-year-old is a nice break for me but is too long a gap between sessions for her. Once I understood the issues I was not so angry and was pleased to be asked my opinion. (Parent of a baby, two-year-old and 4-year-old, January 2008)

Staff views

Staff professed an overall view that it makes a difference having a multidisciplinary senior management leadership team which helped break down professional barriers; a not unexpected perspective from different disciplines who had elected to work at an integrated centre. Least expected was a view that doing so dissipated their expertise. For example:

> Being part of a multi-disciplinary team has streamlined how we do things and gives a seamless service to parents. We understand all aspects of family life and see children in a holistic way. Nothing is left out. We have a clearer picture of what goes on in families. (Teacher, February 2008)

> The more agencies are involved the better the chances of positive outcomes because there is greater experience, knowledge and resources. (Early Years Practitioner, February 2008)

> I am thinking about families and children in a different way because of all the different viewpoints. (Early Years Assistant, February 2008)

> Different disciplines have a slightly different focus so having a multidisciplinary approach ensures all outcomes are covered. (Community Family Worker, February 2008)

> There is a common framework for planning and assessment and record keeping for a smoother transition through the groups especially Tiny Tots to Nursery. (Teacher, February 2008)

However, a number had differing opinions on integrated working. These are reoccurring threads in the pattern of everyday working and can be summed up by the following examples. Firstly, from the educationalists:

> The curriculum is lost in multi-agency working. Education is watered down. Where will it end? (Headteacher, November 2007)

> The curriculum has been hijacked. All we talk about at staff meetings at school are extended schools, after school clubs and the Common Assessment Framework (CAF). We don't talk about how to help children learn. (Teacher, January 2008)

From the health professionals:

> I feel our role as Health Visitors has changed tremendously – we are told not to do things we used to do and to target hard to reach groups and I wonder why I did my qualifications because I am told other people can do what I used to do. (Health Visitor, March 2008)

These are not new sentiments and have been well documented in other research studies on multi-agency working (Anning and Edwards 2006; Anning et al., 2006; Aubrey, 2007). However, different views emerged as the research focused upon how integrated working brought about direct benefits to children and families. There was a consensus that the centre was a learning community and education is at the heart of all that is done – from the smallest baby – to the oldest grandparent. For example:

> One of the impacts of integrated planning has been that all sessions are now planned. 'Bumps and Babes' for example have been working with parents on messy play. Today they had a session where the babies played with the jelly. I don't know who enjoyed it more – the babies or the parents! (Community Family Worker, March 2008)

> What do we mean by education? As a learning community, surely all that we do is education? (Teacher, March 2008)

> Perhaps there is nothing now that sits purely in health or education or social care. Everything we do uses all aspects and has a knock on effect. To put the services into different categories now is creating artificial boundaries. (Family Services Manager, March 2008)

Building trust

This collective reflection of views became much more than a series of statements about aspects of practice. To categorise them as being positive or negative was far too simplistic. They became a means of returning to those most closely involved, asking how they saw joined-up services. The response was interesting. It revealed that services were joined least by what professionals did for parents but by developing and forging trust between professionals and between parents and professionals. Figure 8.1 represents an organisational picture of the responses as a jigsaw. Children and families are at the heart of the process although integrated working is not wholly in place. The jigsaw interlocks at certain points but does not yet represent a seamless transition of services and expertise.

However, what is significant is that there is no representation of who provides which services. This is because different professional groups appear to have focused on the service rather than who (in terms of professional role) performs that service. A view prompted by a group discussion about the way the centre implemented the five outcomes from *Every Child Matters* (DCSF, 2008). One person said.

> There is no pure education, social or health here at the centre anymore. Everything is interlinked. The five outcomes of ECM are the glue holding the services together. (Family Services Manager, April 2008)

They went on to say 'the most important ingredient of the glue is trust'. Another said:

> Trust enables shared understanding thus reducing the likelihood of a clash of expectations and priorities which will not support the child. Relationships with trust are more likely to develop into partnerships with parents. (Health Visitor, April 2008)

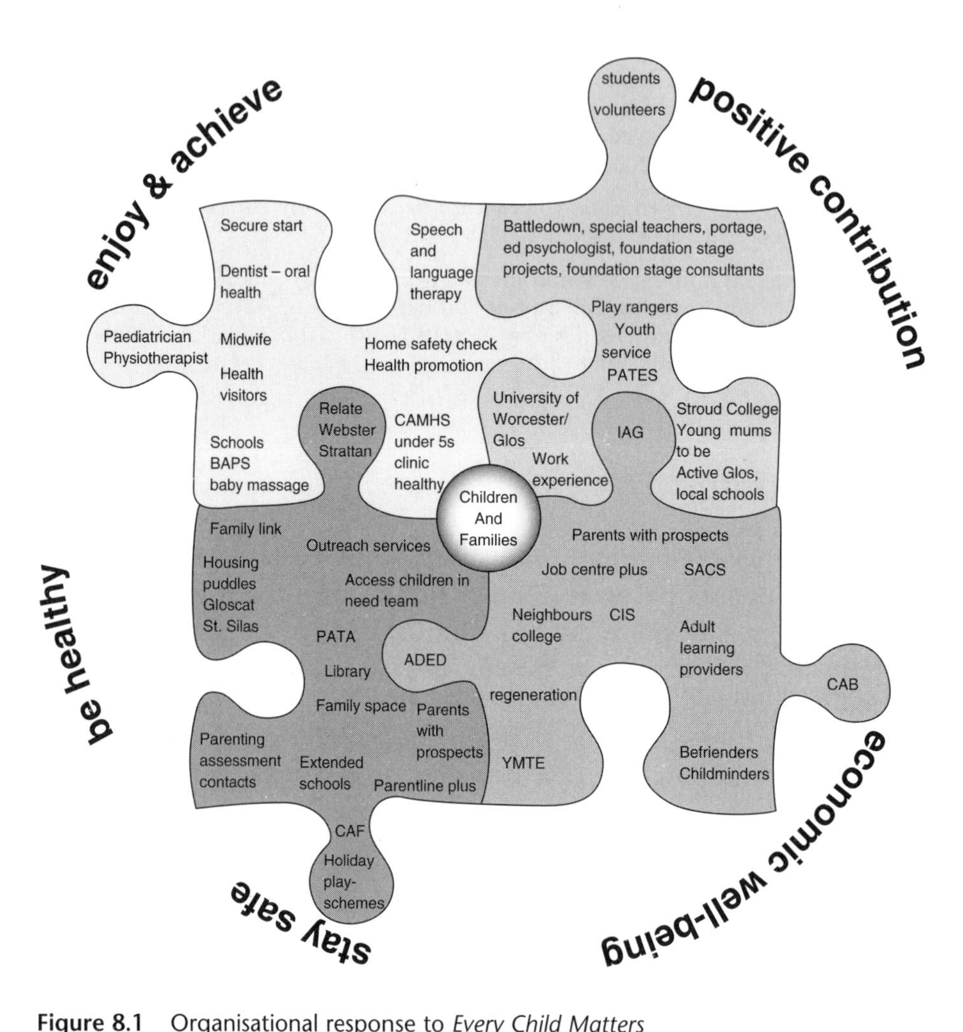

Figure 8.1 Organisational response to *Every Child Matters*

These views seemed to resonate with the views of parents. They suggested trust is the reason they feel able to take up services. For example, they know their Health Visitor will be at the centre running a class for parents. An outreach worker is also an Early Years Practitioner at their child's nursery session and she will be running the parenting training course. A Tiny Tots session has inspired them to start learning at an adult learning course at the centre. The Cook has shown a parent how to provide a healthy meal on a budget and they want to volunteer to help in the kitchen. The Community Family Worker who visits them at home also runs the crèche for their child while they attend a literacy course. It is not a matter of just knowing those involved; it becomes more about trusting those involved.

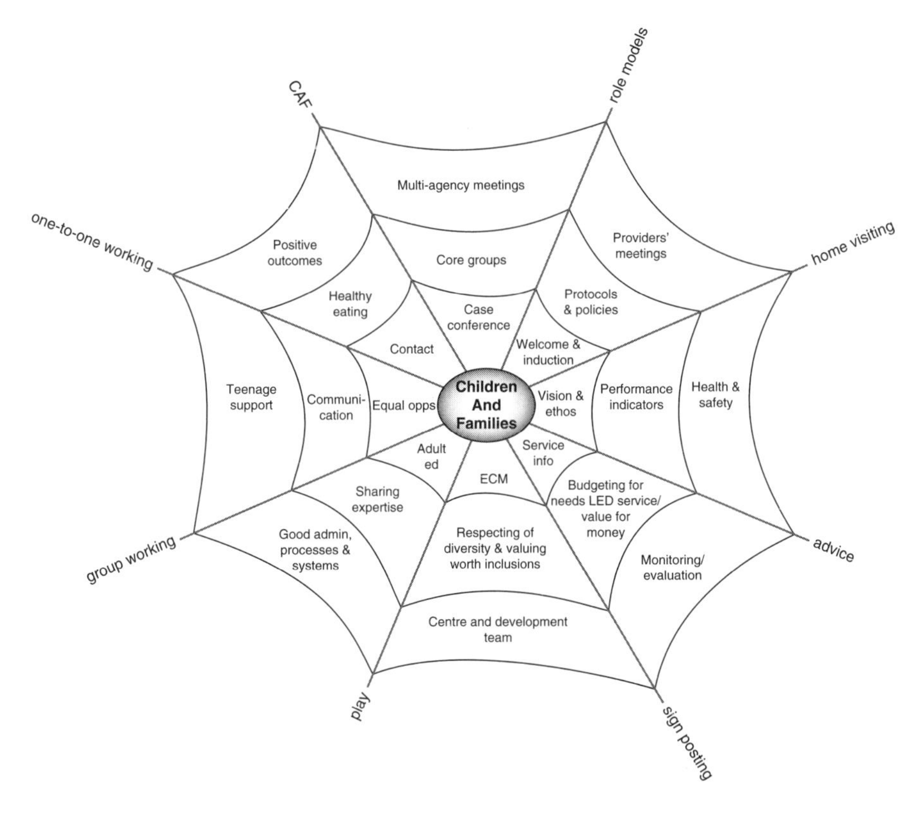

Figure 8.2 Model of integrated working

What does this tell us about integrated working?

It is now possible to look in detail at the jigsaw model reproduced as Figure 8.1. Some staff have been at the centre for some time and were able to consider their own professional heritage and experience. They compared the provision of services today with a time (before Sure Start) when the work strands were clearly demarcated into Health, Education and Social Care. This allowed a useful means of reflecting upon how much has developed and changed over the years. It was clear they felt placing services into different categories, for example Health and Social Work was outmoded and would immediately create artificial boundaries. They moved on to consider whether the model represented in Figure 8.1 should be refined in such a way as to more clearly indicate the model of integrated working taking place and to an extent to what the centre has aspired. Staff devised a model of integrated working which is shown as Figure 8.2. The model is represented as a spider's web. This shows the services at the centre as interweaving threads which make up a web or net that protects the child and her family, and was described as 'a net, which no child should slip through'. Eight strands make up the systems which underpin integrated working at the centre.

The team felt the threads and strands also represented an interesting analogy in that they could be broken but easily rebuilt – thus representing the interaction between professionals and parents; and acknowledging that sometimes the relationship could be fragile, but always supportive. The web also represents the way professionals support each other in order to make a strong structure for integrated working. There was some concern that using this analogy and the 'web diagram' might be seen as a gimmick and a way of presenting a pretty picture of what went on. However, there was a strongly held view that the 'web diagram' and using the spider's web analogy allowed a description of support and ways of building confidence which could be easily understood by parents. Importantly, the language used to describe the model is not mere jargon taken from different professions but words with which everyone can identify, the team felt.

> This represents the service we would wish to see for our parents and children. A way of indicating the robustness of the professionals involved to withstand stress and change in order to provide a high quality service. (Children's Centre Team, February 2008)

Point for reflection

The image can be likened to a spider's web which is made of strong silk and can withstand a great deal of pressure before it breaks.

> Spider silk is extremely strong and is on weight basis stronger than steel. It has been suggested that a pencil thick strand of silk could stop a Boeing 747 in flight. (University of Bristol, 2002: online)

Spider silk is waterproof, elastic and has immunity to decay and decomposition by bacteria, which make it resilient – properties which in many ways describe the resilience and strength needed at the centre. These qualities are also essential to teach children independence, develop skills and promote resilience. Spider webs are twice as elastic as nylon and this potential allows for flexibility within the model. Ask yourself, how true is this when considering a

(Continued)

(Continued)

Children's Centre? Many forces can interplay to cause destruction of emerging partnerships and fragility of parents with complex, endemic issues to overcome. The smallest to the largest spider can make a web. Leadership can come from different professionals, parents and children at different times. It is not a hierarchical structure and is without layers. More strands may be added, and it can bend and be flexible; it can resist being damaged from time to time.

It is now possible to see how the process of listening to those most closely involved has allowed this view of practice to emerge. The analogy of the spider's web follows through to the strategic plans for the centre set by the Senior Management Team. The strands weave into all aspects of the organisation, including budget, human resource development, objective setting and performance management – indeed, all decision-making at an everyday level. It is a system of movement, evolution and careful management.

Point for reflection

- Is listening to those most closely involved a means of reflecting on practice?
- How is it possible to prove that the views are indeed valid?
- Are they reliable?
- Are they representative?
- Do they really inform practice?

There is no doubt that listening to those most closely involved has allowed people to articulate what they were already doing. That is, creating new ways of developing professional partnerships aimed at meeting the needs of families. It has also allowed people to answer questions, have their views listened to and reflect on what contribution they make. The process mirrors what Ryde (2007) considers important ways of reflecting on practice and leads to people developing 'above and beyond questions' and teasing out different models of practice. They also begin to do what Bolton (2001) considers an important aspect of reflection, that is, formulating their own questions about the situations in which they find themselves. Indeed, just listening and finding out was a starting point to improve practice. It is clear that services have changed and evolved. Parents now seem to know intuitively what to expect as the centre becomes increasingly integrated with the community. They are moving away from an expectation that they are likely to receive a Health, Social Care or Education model of service delivery. They experience a personalised approach to meeting their needs, though this takes time and requires professionals to organise ways of identifying parents' needs. This is sometimes problematic because parents are reluctant to participate in parent forums and governance meetings. This is why it is important for parents to become an integral part of the process of shaping needs-led services. They need to trust the integration of services and develop a relationship with staff who can either provide the service themselves or who can signpost them to services which can be delivered locally and speedily. Indeed, parents and professionals are developing skills needed in the home and the workplace. What is more, professionals are transferring these skills into the home and parents are using them to support families and gain employment.

Summary

Listening to those most closely involved was not intended to encompass the embodiment of knowledge in practice. It did however start to unpack knowledge and generated a means of reflecting on practice. It took a snapshot of practice as this chapter represents only part of the research. The whole photograph album contains the skills of leaders, practitioners, parents and children. It is these people who will move forward this developing view of integrated working. They are the people who are most closely involved; what is important is that they are heard.

Suggested further reading

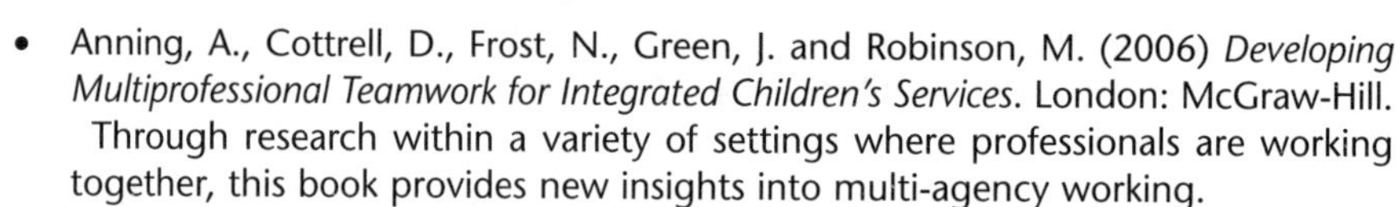

- Anning, A., Cottrell, D., Frost, N., Green, J. and Robinson, M. (2006) *Developing Multiprofessional Teamwork for Integrated Children's Services*. London: McGraw-Hill.
  Through research within a variety of settings where professionals are working together, this book provides new insights into multi-agency working.

- Aubrey, C. (2007) *Leading and Managing in the Early Years.* London: Sage Publications.
  This book explores leadership in children's centres and gives practical advice as well as underpinning principles, theory and research evidence.

- Whalley, M. (2006) 'Children's centres: the new frontier for the welfare state and education system?', paper presented at Early Interventions for Infants and Small Children conference, Grand Hotel Oslo, Norway.
  This paper gives an inspiring vision of the work of children's centres and what they are setting out to achieve with families, parents and children. It discusses integrated working within children's centres.

References

Anning, A. and Edwards, A. (2006) *Promoting Children's Learning from Birth to Five: Developing the New Early Years Professional.* 2nd edn. Maidenhead: Open University Press.

Anning, A., Cottrell, D., Frost, N., Green, J. and Robinson, M. (2006) *Developing Multiprofessional Teamwork for Integrated Children's Services.* London: McGraw-Hill

Aubrey, C. (2007) *Leading and Managing in the Early Years.* London: Sage Publications.

Bolton, G. (2001) *Reflective Practice.* London: Paul Chapman Publishing.

Department for Children, Schools and Families (DCSF) (2008) 'Every Child Matters: outcomes for children and young people'. http://www.everychildmatters.gov.uk/aims/outcomes/ (accessed 15.01.2009).

Department of the Environment, Transport and the Regions (DETR) (2000) 'Incidences of Deprivation 2000: Regeneration Research Summary Number 31'. http://www.communities.gov.uk/archived/publications/citiesandregions/indices derivation (accessed 22.01.2009).

Ryde, R. (2007) *Thought Leadership: Moving Hearts and Minds.* London: Palgrave Macmillan.

University of Bristol (2002) 'Spider silk properties: uses and production'. www.chm.bris.ac.uk/motm/spider/page2.htm (accessed 22.01.2009).

9

Managing Multi-agency Working

Wendy Messenger

Chapter objectives

In this chapter I argue that the central reason for pursuing an innovative, difficult and often complex agenda of interagency working is because:

> Children do not distinguish their needs based on which agencies run which services – neither should we. (DfES, 2004: 20)

We need to remind ourselves of this quotation when times get tough. It is what motivates me to continue to believe this is the right way forward. In order to understand where we are today, we (as professionals) need to understand where we have come from and what the journey has been like along the way. I feel this has evolved via a response to a number of different agendas, namely:

- protecting children;
- addressing issues of social disadvantage and inequality;
- associated factors of educational underachievement and poor health and well-being;
- enabling parents back to work;
- a radical reform and modernisation of public services.

What do we mean by multi-agency working?

An abundance of terminology has developed to describe this way of working, for example:

- partnership working;
- multi-agency working;
- integrated working;
- collaborative working;
- interprofessional working.

As Anning et al. (2006) acknowledge, this has led to confusion. Frost (2005), Atkinson et al. (2005) and Pascal et al. (1999) have all offered definitions, models and analyses. Lloyd et al. (2001) offer somewhat straightforward definitions:

> **Multi-agency working**: more than one agency working together with a young person, family or project but not necessarily jointly. Often the terms multi-agency and interagency are used interchangeably.
>
> **Interagency working**: more than one agency working together in a planned and formal way.
>
> **Joint working**: when professionals from more than one agency work together on a project, for example speech and language therapists, and early years workers delivering group work.
>
> **Integrated working** focuses on 'enabling and encouraging professionals to work together to adopt common processes to deliver front line services, coordinated and built around the needs of children and young people' (McInnes, 2007: 9).

Why is multi-agency working so important in the early years?

The *Every Child Matters* Green Paper (DfES, 2003) acknowledged that too many children were falling through the cracks between different services, which meant they were being failed to be protected from risk of harm or neglect. Too often children experienced difficulties at home or at school but received too little help, too late, once problems had reached crisis point. Intervening early is now seen as paramount and processes have been developed to ensure this is possible, including:

- improving information sharing between agencies;
- the development of a Common Assessment Framework (CAF) to ensure information is collected and shared across services;
- introducing a lead professional to ensure a coherent package of services can be put in place to meet the needs of the child and family;
- the development of 'on the spot' service delivery whereby professionals will be encouraged to work together in multidisciplinary teams based in and around schools and children's centres. Sure Start children's centres are considered to be the main vehicle for providing good quality integrated services to children under 5. They offer a seamless and integrated service by providing a 'one stop shop' for the provision of services to children and families.

Formerly, children and their families accessed services individually, resulting in somewhat piecemeal provision. The crux of multi-agency working is based on the premise that 'two or more heads are better then one'. Professionals, by sharing their expertise and making decisions based on their shared knowledge, are able to meet children's needs more effectively.

Point for reflection

Who are the professionals that might make up your multi-agency team?

- Early Years worker;
- Teacher;
- Speech and Language Therapist;
- Family Support Worker;
- Health Visitor;
- Midwife;
- Community Development Worker;
- Social Worker;
- Substance Misuse Worker;
- GP;
- Psychologist;
- Psychiatrist.

In fact, it could be any professional linked with health, community work, social care, and education, and could include professionals from the voluntary sector, for example, Scope or Barnado's. Parents/carers are also often invited to participate in decisions around the nature and extent of services that are offered. The *Common Core of Knowledge and Skills for the Children's Workforce* (DfES, 2005), the first official publication of requirements, does not actually specify which agencies or professionals should be involved; perhaps this is because there is a need to step away from titles and professions and think more about what is to be done rather than who does it. The *Every Child Matters* website states that:

> Multi agency working has been shown to be an effective way of supporting children and young people with additional needs and securing real improvements in their life outcomes. (DCSF, 2008: online)

Bertram et al. (2002) in their evaluation of early excellence centres found that interagency working contributes to high-quality services for children and families. The Effective Early Learning project (Sylva et al., 2003) also found that in integrated settings where professionals were working together they produced the best quality early years practice and this was directly associated with higher intellectual/cognitive and social behavioural development in children. The Children's Workforce Development Council Report (CWDC, 2007) and the National Audit Office report (2006) both acknowledge that whilst there is still work to be done, there is evidence that this way of working is having a positive impact on outcomes for children and families.

Requirements for multi-agency working

Knowledge and understanding of one's own role as well as those of others is crucial to interagency working according to McInnes (2007) because it is easy for working roles to become blurred or confused. It is important to know what is expected of you and what you can expect from others so that each can contribute effectively to the team. Acknowledging each other's strengths is also seen to be a positive factor. Multi-agency working is often complex due to a coming together of different organisational and professional cultures and working practices. This may lead to difficulties related to a persons' role, understanding the professional language of others, and ensuring responsibility and accountability of team members. It would seem, therefore, that successful multi-agency working requires close attention to the following areas:

1. Communication

In almost every study related to multi-agency working, communication is cited as a factor that can enhance working in this way, or become a barrier. McInnes suggests there are three aspects to this:

- communication skills;
- providing opportunities for dialogue;
- information dissemination.

Bertram et al. (2002), Frost (2005) and Myers et al. (2004) all cite the need for a common language and warn against the use of professional jargon which has the potential to exclude some staff.

2. Leadership

Effective leadership is vital in order to drive a clear vision and overcome the many complex challenges of interagency working. Leadership in the early years is increasingly being seen as important.

Leadership is not just important for managers; it is important that everyone working in this field is a leader. This concurs with Harris (2007) who supports the notion of 'distributed leadership', which recognises there are multiple leaders and that leadership activities need to be widely shared within organisations. Wenger et al. (2002: 123) suggest that distributed forms of leadership are required 'to cross multiple types of boundaries and to share ideas and insights'.

3. Joint training

There is much evidence that joint training enhances multi-agency working through greater understanding of roles and responsibilities and team issues. It also helps to facilitate a shared understanding of related theories. Tomlinson (2003) suggests the use of case studies, role play, experiential placements and educational vignettes and work shadowing.

4. Culture

The development of a shared culture based on mutual respect and diversity is reinforced by Frost (2005). This needs to be within individual organisations as well as across organisations. Therefore practitioners need to understand very well the culture of their own organisation before they can begin to understand the culture of others. Wenger et al. (2002) refer to communities of practice where practitioners develop a shared repertoire of 'experiences, stories, tools and ways of solving problems'. This takes time and involves sustained interaction but can lead to a better understanding of different organisational and professional cultures. The Common Core of Knowledge and Skills (DfES, 2005) suggests there are six areas of expertise that need to be developed in people working with children:

- effective communication and engagement;
- child and young person development;
- safeguarding and promoting the welfare of the child;
- supporting transitions;
- multi-agency working;
- sharing information.

Most other Government departments, professional bodies and awarding bodies also refer to *knowledge* and *skills*. It has led me to question what is meant by *knowledge* and *skills*. The following dictionary definitions have been useful:

> **Knowledge** – the state or fact of knowing. Familiarity, awareness, or understanding gained through experience or study.
>
> **Skills** – the ability to do something well, usually gained through training or experience.

During initial and subsequent training much time is spent in developing skills and knowledge, in fact they are always inherent in the criteria for passing a vocational course. Having developed the necessary skills and knowledge, the ability to practise such skills in the field is deemed to have been demonstrated. Indeed, it can be argued that a particular type of skills and knowledge often marked out professions from each other, for example a teacher from a social worker. Of course, it is important there are specific knowledge and skill requirements for each type of professional in order to be able to offer specific expertise within a multi-agency team. However, it is also the case that some knowledge and skills are common to more than one group of professions who work within children's services. This is even more apparent since the development of the *Common Core of Skills and Knowledge for the Children's Workforce* (DfES, 2005). I believe it is just as important for different professions to acknowledge their shared skills and knowledge as it is to recognise their specific areas of expertise. However, in my experience the acquisition of skills and knowledge does not seem to be enough to work in this way; it also requires personal qualities. Again, a dictionary definition is useful here:

> **Qualities** – inherent or distinguishing characteristics, personal character traits. I would describe these as follows:

- high emotional intelligence;
- an ability to see the vision and purpose of the work;
- a willingness to engage with others in joint ventures and training;
- a willingness to evolve with the culture of the multi-professional team;
- resourcefulness;
- a willingness to shed preconceived ideas and share experience.

I would argue that the possession of these personal qualities can and does make the difference between high-quality multi-agency working and patchy, poor quality provision. They are required by everyone, despite their status or profession and are also intrinsic to the development of knowledge and skills. They should not be seen as part of a continuum or hierarchy, or a particular job role; they are very much the building blocks of multi-agency working. Qualities are part of a thread that is woven into all of the ways that Government and researchers perceive multi-agency working. This leads to the question: can these qualities be acquired or are they innate? It is my view some people already possess them to a greater or lesser extent but they can be learned. This raises a key question, which I shall explore later, which is the use of self-reflection with others as a way to develop these qualities.

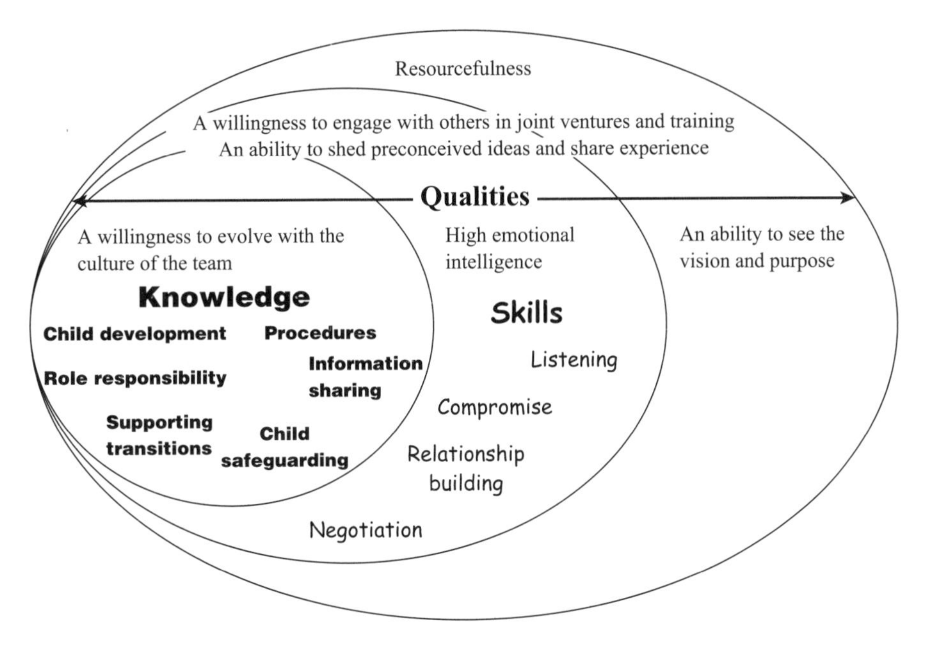

Figure 9.1 Qualities: The threads which draw professionals together

Why should training make a difference?

All children's services are working towards achieving the five outcomes of *Every Child Matters*, therefore developing a common vision at operational level and strategic level is of utmost importance. In order to achieve this, communication and collaboration would seem to be a priority. Atkinson et al. (2002) suggest that listening, negotiation, compromise and building personal relationships are the key communication skills that are required for multi-agency working. The DCSF (2008) support this view and reinforce the importance of bringing teams together to address differences in language and processes in order to develop a common view. Frost (2005) suggests that training can be seen as something that encourages the specific identity of professions and as a process that can encourage joined-up working when undertaken on an interdisciplinary basis. Understanding the roles and responsibilities of other agencies appears to be a key factor to successful multi-agency working. Barr (2003, cited in Frost, 2005) considers that the key components of interprofessional education should be the application of principles of adult learning to interactive group-based learning and there needs to be clear links between collaborative learning and collaborative practice. Whalley et al. (2004) explore the notion of androgogy (how adults learn) and give consideration to:

- the central importance of experience in learning, and that our past experience and present needs are the most important resource for future learning in which participants can give and receive support from colleagues as well as from training leaders/tutors/teachers;

- the creation of a supportive but challenging learning climate in which a strong learning community is established.

Nevertheless, training in multi-agency working is still in its infancy and remains rather patchy but seems to take place to some extent at all levels, including vocational qualifications and some relevant degree programmes. Aspects of multi-agency working are also commonly addressed in the Common Assessment Framework (CAF) training. It is also part of the requirement to be considered for Early Years Professional Status (EYPS) and Qualified Teacher Status (QTS). At the time of writing, an integrated qualifications framework is being developed in which it is hoped integrated working and training to work in multi-agency teams will form the backbone of the framework. Presently, at postgraduate level, there are only a few universities in the UK that offer study in this area. As for those already engaged in training, the situation is perhaps more positive. For example, let us consider a student I have recently supported.

A picture of practice – multi-agency working

Carole was a student who worked as a midwife at a Sure Start children's centre. Through her professional training and practice, she had strong ethical principles, particularly around issues relating to confidentiality. Sharing information with other professionals within the children's centre was new to her. The module was attended by a wide variety of people from different backgrounds, including health and social care, early years and education. One of the activities was to undertake a task collaboratively that culminated in a joint presentation. There was a requirement to reflect on the process, which ultimately became more significant than the final presentation. Schön (1983) suggests we form theories as we reflect on practices that are based on the knowledge we bring from earlier actions or experiences.

(Continued)

(Continued)

Diane was a student who had been reflecting on some issues regarding the quality of service that was being provided by a partner agency. She felt that children and families were suffering as a result and knew she needed to take action but was unsure about the best way of doing so. I reflected on what she had told me and asked questions rather than offered solutions. Diane was able to move from reflection in action towards reflection on action, which subsequently enabled her to decide what her next step would be to resolve the situation.

This type of mentoring, in my experience, empowers people to become more confident and competent leaders. Carole, within her learning community reflected on her professional identity and why maintaining confidentiality was so important to her. She articulated this, whilst at the same time listening to the views of the others within the group. Some of the others had the alternative view; that sharing all information was crucial if multi-agency working was going to be successful and achieve better outcomes for children and families. Etherington (2004) suggests we need to be aware of the personal, social and cultural contexts in which we live and work and to understand how these impact on the ways we interpret our world. This was exactly what Carole was doing as she reflected with the group on how she came to be a midwife, how her experience of training and practice had influenced her beliefs and attitudes, and thus how she had formed her views surrounding confidentiality. Reflecting on this discussion, Carole considered she better understood the debate, the views and practices of other professionals.

In effect what Carole and Diane were doing was to reflect on practice, something that all the training I have been involved with tends to do. This premise is based upon such writers and researchers as Dewey (1933) who describes reflections as the kind of thinking that consists of turning a subject over in the mind and giving it serious thought. Schön (1983) considers the two main processes of professional practice as those of reflection in action and those of reflection on action. Reflection in action is guided by the process of knowledge in use at the time within the specific context; whilst reflection on action occurs afterwards via verbalised or non-verbalised thought and has a role in learning in informing action and theory building. For those involved in multi-agency working it helps to make sense of the complexity of their day-to-day interactions and to support them in moving forward together. Freire (1972) speaks of 'praxis'. He suggests that all human activity consists of action and reflection (praxis) but he maintains it requires theory to illuminate it. How do we do this with people who are training to lead in multi-agency working? Freire goes on to suggest that leaders do bear responsibility for coordination, and at times direction, but they also need to allow others to engage in praxis in order for groups and leaders to grow together. In fact engaging in reflection

(Continued)

(Continued)

within teams and across teams is the process of how individuals and teams grow together.

> No one educates anyone else. Nor do we educate ourselves. We educate one another, in communion, in the context of living in this world. (Freire, 1972: 80)

Indeed this sums up my own experience and the need to examine my own views as a trainer and facilitator of multi-agency working. Since becoming a university lecturer, I have had opportunities to work with colleagues and students from a variety of professional backgrounds. The following, quoted by Freire (1972: 80), sums up the process that seems to have taken place:

> The teacher is no longer merely the one-who-teaches, but one who is himself taught in dialogue with students who in their turn while being taught also teach. They become jointly responsible for the process in which all grow.

Point for reflection

It is important that, for the process of reflection to occur, qualities as well as knowledge and skills need to be developed. Think about how you might:

- build on your own experiences;
- increase your self-awareness;
- create opportunities to become reflective practitioners.

Whilst there are many driving forces for change, including Government policy and initiatives, it would seem these alone will not bring about change in the way people work in a multi-agency environment. It requires professionals to be supported and trained to develop knowledge and skills, but more importantly to develop qualities. In order to develop in this way, when you participate in training you need to consider the following questions:

- Where are you now?
- What are the things that drive forward new ideas and practices?
- Where might you want to be?
- What inherent qualities do you have (or perhaps hold or need to develop)?
- What can you learn from others?
- How might you move forward?

Summary

Nobody I have ever met has said that the *Every Child Matters* agenda is a bad idea. Of course it makes sense for us to be working together to meet the children and families' needs in a more holistic way by pooling our expertise, sharing information and intervening sooner rather than later. Great strides have been made towards this becoming a reality, but there is still much to be done. Anning et al. (2006: 71) note that 'professionals who are working in multi-professional teams are being expected to confront, articulate and lay to one side their long established "tribal beliefs" and behaviours'. Our challenge for the future is to continue to address these issues, and perhaps as Robinson et al. (2008) suggest, this will best be done though reflective processes of confronting difference. The role of training to lead in multi-agency working must surely be in this area and to support leaders to enable it to happen.

It would be naive to propose that successful multi-agency working is purely about the establishment of positive, respectful relationships where every party is clear about their role. There are factors related to the strategic direction of the different organisations, line management structures, pay and conditions of staff and budgetary pressures, to name but a few. All of which influence the opportunities and challenges of multi-agency working.

Quality of service to children and families through multi-agency working will only be improved if we focus on the personal qualities necessary to engage in this type of working. This can only be done by encouraging participants of training to engage in reflection. Additionally, this reflection should be seen as an integrated part of training. Shared reflection with each other helps us to understand better the perspectives of others whilst at the same time helps to develop knowledge, skills and qualities. Without reflection, we are in danger of once again attempting to base multi-agency working around roles and demarcated responsibilities, a practice we know does not support the needs of often the most vulnerable children and families in our society. It is important that whilst continuing to give attention to the processes involved in multi-agency working, we also monitor the impact of those processes. Ongoing evaluation of multi-agency working needs to continue in order that we seek to find ways to support the needs of all children and families in the best way possible.

Suggested further reading

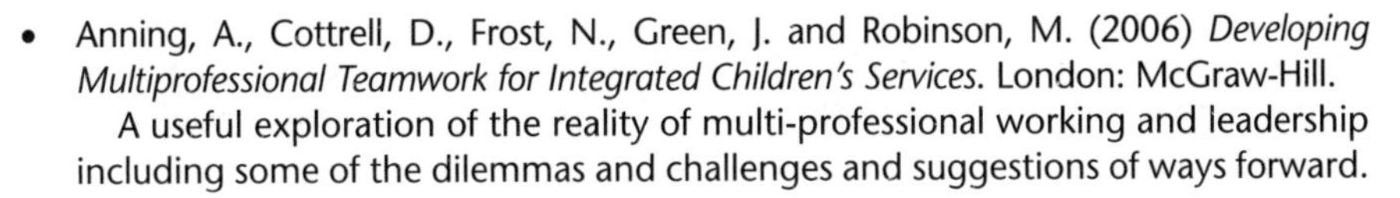

- Anning, A., Cottrell, D., Frost, N., Green, J. and Robinson, M. (2006) *Developing Multiprofessional Teamwork for Integrated Children's Services.* London: McGraw-Hill.
  A useful exploration of the reality of multi-professional working and leadership including some of the dilemmas and challenges and suggestions of ways forward.

- Wenger, E. (1999) *Communities of Practice. Learning, Meaning and Identity*. Cambridge: Cambridge University Press.

  This provides a good understanding of the relationship between learning together and understanding one's own identity. This approach lends itself well to leading multi-agency and multi-professional teams.

References

Anning, A., Cottrell, D., Frost, N., Green, J. and Robinson, M. (2006) *Developing Multiprofessional Teamwork for Integrated Children's Services*. London: McGraw-Hill.

Atkinson, M., Doherty, P. and Kinder, K. (2005) 'Multi-agency working: models, challenges and key factors for success', *Journal of Early Childhood Research*, 3(1): 7–17.

Atkinson, M., Wilkin, A., Stott, A. and Doherty, P. (2002) *Multi-agency Working: A Detailed Study*. Swindon: NFER.

Bertram, T., Pascal, C., Bokhari, S., Gasper, M., Holterman, S., John, K. and Nelson, C. (2002) *Early Excellence Centre Pilot Programme 3rd Annual Evaluation Report 2001–2002*. Birmingham: Centre for Research in Early Childhood.

Children's Workforce Development Council (CWDC) (2007) 'Moving Towards Integrated Working Progress Report'. http://www.cwdcouncil.org.uk/assets/0000/1075/Moving_Towards_Integrated_Working_Progress_Report_Sept07.pdf (accessed 08.01.2009).

Department for Children, Schools and Families (DCSF) (2008) 'Setting up multi-agency services'. http://www.everychildmatters.gov.uk/deliveringservices/multiagencyworking/ (accessed 20.01.2009).

Department for Education and Skills (DfES) (2003) *Every Child Matters*. Green Paper Norwich: TSO.

Department for Education and Skills (DfES) (2004) *Five Year Strategy for Children and Learners: Maintaining Excellent Progress*. Nottingham: DfES.

Department for Education and Skills (DfES) (2005) *Common Core of Skills and Knowledge for the Children's Workforce*. Nottingham: DfES.

Dewey, J. (1933) *The Political Writings*. Indianapolis, IN: Hacket.

Etherington, C. (2004) *Becoming a Reflexive Researcher. Using Our Selves in Research*. London: Jessica Kingsley.

Freire, P. (1972) *Pedagogy of the Oppressed*. London: Penguin.

Frost, N. (2005) *Professionalism, Partnership and Joined-up Thinking. A Research Review of Front Line Working with Children and Families*. Dartington: Research in Practice.

Harris, A. (2007) 'Distributed leadership: conceptual confusion and empirical reticence', *International Journal of Leadership in Education*, 10(3): 1–11.

Lloyd, G., Stead, J. and Kendrick, A. (2001) *Hanging on in There. A Study of Interagency Work to Prevent School Exclusion in Three Local Authorities*. London: National Children's Bureau.

McInnes, K. (2007) *A Practitioner's Guide to Interagency Working in Children's Centres: A Review of the Literature*. London: Barnardo's Policy and Research Unit.

Myers, P., Barnes, J. and Brodie, I. (2004) 'Partnership working in Sure Start local programmes. Synthesis of early findings from local programme evaluations'. www.ness.bbk.ac.uk (accessed 26.01.2009).

National Audit Office (2006) *National Evaluation of Sure Start Children's Centres*. London: HMSO.

Pascal, C., Bertram, T., Gasper, M., Mould, C., Ramsden, F. and Saunders, M. (1999) *Research to Inform the Evaluation of the Early Excellence Centres Pilot Programme*. London: DfEE.

Robinson, M., Atkinson, M. and Downing, D. (2008) *Supporting Theory Building in Integrated Services Research*. London: NFER.

Schön, D. (1983) *The Reflective Practitioner: How Professionals Think in Action*. New York: Basic Books.

Sylva, K., Melhuish, E., Sammons, P., Siraj-Blactchford, I., Taggart, B. and Elliot, K. (2003) *The Effective Provision of Pre-school Education (EPPE) Project: Findings from the Pre-school Period*. London: Institute of Education.

Tomlinson, K. (2003) *Effective Interagency Working: A Review of the Literature and Examples from Practice: LGA Research Report 40*. Swindon: NFER.

Wenger, E., McDermott, R. and Snyder, W. (2002) *Cultivating Communities of Practice*. Cambridge, MA: Harvard Business School Press.

Whalley, M., Whitaker, P., Fletcher, C., Thorpe, S., John, K. and Leisten, R. (2004) *NPQICL Induction Programme: Pen Green Research Development Training Base and Leadership Centre*. Nottingham: NCSL.

Section 4

Positive Relationships in a Multi-agency World

10

Distance Learning and Professional Development

Victoria Cooper

Chapter objectives

This chapter examines research with early years students at the Open University on the impact of reflective thinking and practice on their professional development. It considers the interaction and collaboration the students have with their colleagues and how this supports a community of practice. A central theme of the chapter is how the students feel and respond to change and how talking and writing about their experiences enhances their professional practice. This also demonstrates the importance of student-centred learning.

> I have had to un-learn all that I had learnt before ... It's been quite a journey for me, really stressful sometimes. I suppose I used to just do things without really thinking. Now I question everything – how I see my practice, how I observe has changed. I have become more critical. Not just of my own practice but of those around me. My practice has definitely improved ... I only realise this now. I can see how much I have changed as a practitioner and as a student. (Leanne, 33, early years student)

The opening extract introduces us to Leanne, a mature early years student who is studying for a Foundation Degree through distance learning with the Open University (OU). Leanne was a member of a focus group made up of early years students (EYS) who agreed to discuss their experiences as part of a small-scale research project carried out at the Open University. All of the students were studying at the university and their personal details have been changed to provide anonymity. Their stories, however, are presented in their own words. In the extract, Leanne introduces the notion of a 'journey' and the elements that she felt were important – as well as learning from her journey. She indicates how she has changed as a result and the impact that this has had upon her professional practice. The extract is therefore a starting point for what follows and offers us a glimpse of her experiences. We will listen to Leanne again later and listen to others some with similar and some with different experiences to share.

Whilst we were keen to examine student experiences we did not anticipate the impact that our reflective research process would have upon participants. Reflection has emerged as a significant theme, both as a feature of student experiences, but also implicit within the research process. This allows us to present a model of how reflection in practice can work. The process we used built upon previous research exploring learning within a higher education context (Lea, 2005) and the impact of organisational features and course design (Rogers, 2000). Using student experiences we examine learning through interaction, noting collaboration and reflection as instruments for development.

The data we gathered was further interpreted using the work of Lave and Wenger (1991) and Wenger (1998) and their contribution to an analysis of informal learning. This had a particular focus on the way communities of practice can emerge when groups of individuals come together to share experiences, learn or evolve strategies for enhancing their own development. Throughout the chapter extracts from student voices are used to represent learning journeys. This reinforces the importance of encouraging reflection and introduces the concept of a community of practice as a model for exploration.

A picture of practice: the research enquiry

Four key *interrelated* themes emerged from the research. All revolved around a central component, namely, change. These can be seen as:

- responding to changes in early years practice;
- responding to change in role, responsibilities and relationships;

(Continued)

(Continued)

- responding to being a student and developing the ability to engage in reflective thinking;
- responding to change and becoming part of a community of practice.

To 'unpack' these themes the research process built upon a reflexive, story-telling dynamic. This method of gathering and sharing experience is widely used within qualitative fields in education, particularly associated with written narratives (Bruner, 1990), and reflective and diary accounts of experience (Allard et al., 2007). The aim was to create an environment that allows those most closely involved to freely articulate their experiences. In doing so, we were at pains not to direct participants or lead them to focus on any particular area, so minimising the impact we had upon the research process. However, we cannot deny our influence in terms of how we have used each extract as a means to interpret and demonstrate our findings.

Within the traditions of qualitative, ethnographic exploration, a key component within the research was an emphasis upon reflection. This is because to tell and recount stories a high level of reflection was necessary. This builds upon reflective enquiry which has been widely used in education (Bolton, 2006) and medicine (Horowitz et al., 2003) to demonstrate the value of talking and writing as a vehicle to enhance professional practice through reflection. A key feature of ethnographic research is the strong emphasis upon social context which is recognised as imperative to capturing a clear representation of experience (Thomas, 1993). This was a guiding element within our research. The social background and context of each participant cannot therefore be suspended, but is presented within a case study focus. This was intended to illicit 'thick description' (Geertz, 1973) of experience. We acknowledge that qualitative case studies can take a variety of forms, including historical, psychological, ethnographic, and sociological approaches. For the purposes of our research, ethnographic data-gathering instruments have been used, particularly unstructured interviews, focus groups and field notes to help us build up a case study or picture of practice. The approach was underpinned by the work of Lave and Wenger (1991) who explored learning across various informal situations and developed the concept of a community of practice to describe how learning occurs through practice.

According to Wenger (1998) the four basic aspects of practice, including meaning, community, learning and identity, each interact to promote development. Rather than explore learning potentials within formal educational contexts, Wenger presents learning as a social process which evolves through participation and engagement within community social interaction. In this way Wenger highlights how effective learning occurs as much outside as well as inside formal learning environments and directs us to the importance of the process of learning rather than the acquisition of knowledge and skills. In this sense, learning is presented as the curriculum.

(Continued)

(Continued)

Wenger (1998) examines how groups gain access to a given 'community' and so move from the periphery, as novice, to the centre of the group with full group membership. A number of essential ingredients are necessary in order for this transition to take place. These include an initial desire to change and develop group norms and normative behaviour as a means to bind a group together, and to participate in group collaboration, sharing and social interaction in order to reflect upon practice and change. Wenger considers that it is through such a complex process that learning occurs. In this way, participants change as a result of their reflections and learning.

Point for reflection

You may be considering a small-scale enquiry as part of your own professional development.

- Will it have the aim of listening to those most closely involved and interpreting their personal or professional journeys?
- You may decide to seek the views of parents, about an aspect of provision or their views on children's needs.
- You may decide to consult early years practitioners or other professional groups.

Considering the approach as described in this chapter may provide you with ideas about ways to gather information, interpret the views of others, gain insight, and encourage reflection.

Responding to changes in early years practice

An overriding component within the research (as revealed by those involved) was the emphasis upon change as a motivating factor for deciding to study with the OU. Change was seen in a variety of forms, including the desire to change and improve practice, the motivation necessary for change, including aspects of individual identity and, finally, coerced change. Consider these student voices:

> Now I am doing my Foundation Degree I think Jane listens to me more and takes me more seriously. I am not just the dinner lady anymore. (Charlotte, 30, EYS)

We are introduced here to Charlotte, an experienced practitioner working in a local primary school. Charlotte describes how she has changed by focusing on how her identity has shifted. Previously, Charlotte described in detail how she felt a certain degree of pressure in the amount of training she was required to take. She suggests:

> I have worked with Jane, the reception teacher, for three years and before that I worked part-time for two years in year 2. So all in all I have worked in this school for five years. They know me well. Before that I was a dinner lady and helped out at play times. I enjoy my work now much more than before. We have loads of training in school. Some of it is OK, on child protection and curriculum development, but, well, lots of it doesn't even relate to me and I still have to do it. We had an afternoon on children's social and emotional development – it was a waste of time. I don't plan those sort of things, circle time. I don't even do them. I would have liked more time on what I do in class day in day out. There is no point otherwise.

The perceived imposition of training and a strong emphasis upon continuing professional development (CPD) emerged as a key theme as the following extract with Leanne, a 33-year-old foundation degree student who works full-time at a nursery, demonstrates.

> My manager said that I had to do this course – the Foundation Degree. I haven't a NVQ or anything and she said that we had to have a qualification or we would lose our job, so, well I had no choice.

Leanne's account reflects the dilemma faced by some practitioners. They may not see the need for additional training or have the time. This perception supports the findings by Hustler et al. (2003) who describe practitioner resistance to professional development which is often perceived as lacking relevance to their own practice and fails to take into consideration their existing knowledge and experience. Whilst a degree of coerced change appeared, this was very much balanced by the consistent emphasis upon the need for change and improved practice, as Lisa clearly describes:

> Why does CPD matter ... coz it does. My professional development affects the lives of kids and that's what it is all about. How could it not matter? (Lisa, 29, EYS)

Here we are introduced to Lisa, a 29-year-old Foundation Degree (FDEY) student. Lisa works full-time at a private nursery and has done so for the last five years. Her emphasis upon professional development lies at the heart of the many changes in recent provision. Historically, the provision of quality early years practice across different settings has been varied (Siraj-Blatchford et al., 2008) and the patterns of ongoing professional development have been diverse and, in many cases, poorly received by practitioners (Robson, 2008).

However, all respondents emphasised the value of CPD, to themselves, their professional competence and as a response to change.

> Some kids have few chances in life and we like to think that we can make a difference. It's the one stable thing that many of them have. In order to keep up-to-date we need training and skill development – how else can we improve? (Sam, 31, EYS)

Sam, who works with Lisa, is also registered for the FDEY. Sam highlights, in a similar way to Lisa, the importance of early years practice and the value of training. Despite acknowledging the importance of professional development (CPD), there was concern about keeping abreast of recent changes. Leanne exemplifies this view:

> I find it hard to keep up with all the changes. Moving to the birth to three matters framework was quite a change. We had just got to grips with that and then it's all change again. We have started to implement early years foundation stage. It's frustrating, as there have been so many changes. I didn't really want to study. I can see now how important it is, but at the time, well, I have worked in early years for five years, I am experienced. I didn't see the need for studying – I don't have the time. I work full-time and have three young children. As a single Mum it's hard to keep on top of things.

This reveals what can be called a tension between feeling coerced and having the time to study, and recognising training as an important aspect of improving provision. The balance between wanting to study and recognising the importance of CPD is tenuous and reflects the many factors which are important when choosing to study.

> I didn't really want to study but, well I have enjoyed it. It's helped me to change. I can focus now and I feel like I really know something about what I do, not just the everyday stuff, but well, the nitty gritty of how children learn. I have really developed that side of my practice.

This extract signals a degree of pride in the opportunities that training can offer. Listen to Tina, a 26-year-old student who works full-time in a pre-school setting:

> Things have really started to happen for me now. I think I have changed. I have got my NVQ 4 and am doing my Foundation Degree. It's been a hard slog, but I do enjoy it. It makes me feel like a professional. I can talk to our manager and I feel she will listen. I am now as qualified as her. I may not be as experienced, but I am qualified. It's been a great opportunity for me. I feel like I could go on. I would like to be a manager some day.

Her views underline the value the Government now places on professional development. These include a series of policy initiatives designed to promote the role of the Early Years Professional (EYP) in all children's centres by 2010 and in every full day-care setting by 2015. These developments are built upon a clear assertion that improving the professional context of early years work will in turn increase the quality of experience for young children. Another participant, called Charlotte describes both the value and limitations of policy reform within the early years sector. She suggests:

> I agree that things did need to change. Every Child Matters taught us that. But the speed and amount of change has been immense. Just as you get to grips with one thing it then changes. Luckily we have been implementing the Early Years Foundation Stage for a while. Although it is a change, it really only builds upon what we were doing before.

This illustrates a responsiveness to change and the speed of change, but also the importance that is now placed upon practitioners needing to keep abreast of changes in policy and provision. There is now even greater demand to achieve qualifications. For example, a Graduate Funding initiative has now emerged to encourage recruitment and development within the sector. This has necessitated new training provision to be designed for those who wish to take advantage of these initiatives. The Open University responded with the development of a programme of vocational, work-based study, to support early years professional development through a route that allows practitioners to gain a Certificate in Early Years Practice, which is part of the Qualifications Framework identified by the Children's Workforce and Development Council. This leads to a modular route that takes a student to a Foundation Degree in Early Years.

Responding to being a student and developing the ability to engage in reflective thinking

All of those involved in the research were Open University students. The Open University has evolved to become the largest university in the United Kingdom. Currently, there are more than 180,000 students. They are linked to the university via specially produced course materials that are sent to each student. They follow a course calendar and, if they wish, attend occasional group tutorials as well as being connected by computer online at home. They are in fact studying (albeit with the audiovisual trappings of modern society) at a distance, but have in common the same materials, study opportunities and a subject tutor that supports their learning. The OU does not have a student campus but has 12 regional centres throughout the

UK, Scotland, Wales and Northern Ireland. Each regional centre is responsible for facilitating student support, advice, and guidance. Susan, a faculty manager within the university, describes the process:

> Distance learning with the Open University is not fixed to a place. It is not campus based like many universities. It is now an e-learning environment where students can access course information, books and library resources all on-line. Students still receive their course books through the post so that they can study at home, at their own pace. It's a very dynamic model of learning. The OU have created a community for learning. (Susan, 55, faculty manager)

The emphasis upon community and student-centred learning share many features with Lave and Wenger's (1991) view of a community of practice. We can see the many possibilities within OU study to draw a range of diverse groups together, each with varying degrees of experience and knowledge. Rather than being tied to a particular setting, the OU presents a vast learning community which can be accessed online anywhere and at any time, as Veronica, a central academic for the university describes:

> The Open University is committed as an institution to providing learning opportunities for anyone who wishes to study. Now that is unique. Now by providing open access it welcomes a whole host of students from diverse backgrounds and brings them together as a community. It attracts all levels of expertise and experience. (Veronica, 50, central academic)

The emphasis upon diversity is an important guiding feature within the OU both in terms of age, experience, background and expertise. Rather than exclude or select, the OU promotes open access and celebrates diversity. Indeed, the importance of drawing diverse experience together is recognised as a key feature of developing a community of practice (Palincsar et al., 1998; Wenger, 1998). As Veronica explains:

> The OU is good at bringing different groups of students together. Most students are assigned to a tutor as part of a regional tutorial group. This is often a smallish group where students are supported by their tutor in sharing their experiences and material. All our students have access to e-learning materials, on-line library facilities, journals, websites etc. They also each have their set of course materials which are still hard copy. Now this is their opportunity to engage both with the material and with other students. We don't make them. It's entirely up to them.

The work-based element places a strong emphasis upon independent learning and learning through reflection. It draws the workplace and learning context together in an attempt to promote reflective practice. Indeed, reflectivity has become an accepted practice in the field of education and very much assumes a model for improvement and development (Wesley and Buysse, 2001). However, in the case of the students who participated in the focus groups, they were not only required to study at a distance, but all of the respondents were 'returners' to education and each had a particular view of ways to access higher education via distance learning processes:

> I hadn't studied anything since school. That was over fifteen years ago. It was really scary and I didn't want to fail. Once my materials arrived and I had my tutor details, it felt like, well where do I start? (Leanne, 33, EYS)

Leanne was not alone in being a 'returner' to education after many years. She shared this experience with the others. Whilst three of the students had trained and gained further qualifications since leaving school, including NVQ level 3 and 4 and Higher Learning and Teaching Assistant (HLTA), they did not consider these qualifications to demand formal studying. All discussed the difficulties of studying after so many years. Sam developed this point to highlight how she needed additional support to get started.

> When my materials arrived I felt excited, but also a bit scared. I didn't really know what to do with the materials. At first I just looked at them and was too frightened to write or make any notes on them. It wasn't until I went to my second tutorial and saw what everyone else was doing that I realised that they were mine and I could do what I wanted with them. I know that sounds silly. But I hadn't studied for over ten years and even at school I had never made notes or used books in this way. Eventually I had a special session with my tutor who helped me, well gave me a few tips on how to study. It was an absolute eye opener to me. It's all really simple stuff, how to read and make notes and how to highlight. But, well no one had ever shown me before.

Sam's experience indicates where many students start on their journey. As returners to education, many have limited study skills and lack confidence in actually knowing where to start. This might have created a barrier to their learning had it not been for the role of their tutor, and it was the tutor who became a central figure in 'steering' them through the OU support network. Lisa emphasises this point:

> My tutor helped me make sense of everything. There is lots to read and it's hard to know how and where to start. She showed me what to read and how. She also steered me through the OU system, which is quite something in itself. It has a huge database with lots of bits. It's a new language for me. We had a tutor group conference and a national conference. I had never been into a conference before. She helped me find it and made it look pretty easy.

Students were also helped by each other and being part of a group with a shared view of practice and learning. They all participated in different ways exploring various interacting elements of practice that need to evolve within the group before full participation is established and learning can take place. Wenger (1998) stresses the importance of community normative behaviour in which the group take on a distinct identity with their own norms and language which dictate membership. All students stressed the role of their tutor in helping them find their way into their community for learning (perhaps themselves as part of that community of learning). They further highlight the importance of other students and practitioners in assisting learning through collaboration. In this way, we heard how students changed from novice 'returners' to education to more collaborative and active learners.

Changes in role, responsibilities, and relationships

> There was a change in who I was at school. They all knew me as the dinner lady before. Now I was actually supporting their children in class ... well I was different to them, I realised how far I had come – from the dinner lady to practitioner. (Charlotte, 30, EYS)

It is not clear from Charlotte's extract whether her perceived shift in identity actually reflected how parents and others perceived her new role or whether this reflected her own self-belief. The important message within this is how it made Charlotte feel.

> I felt more important I suppose. It was nice that parents seamed [*sic*] to value what I said and that my opinion was important.

Charlotte used this example to demonstrate how much she learned from this, particularly in relation to 'listening' skills, as she describes:

> I never really thought about, well how important it is for someone to listen to you. I know it's important to listen to children, but now, well experiencing this myself has made it clearer.

Similarly, Leanne discusses the importance of listening and uses a learning incident to define this as a light-bulb moment within her learning journey:

> Carey, one of my children, well, she brought in a book – 'The queen's knickers'. She was so excited, cos it was a bit rude. Well she desperately wanted me to read it and I said I would later. I feel really bad because I forgot. I was so busy doing other stuff that I hadn't listened to her and registered how important it was for her. I still feel bad about it.

Leanne's light-bulb moment struck a chord with the group as they all felt the full impact and acknowledged the significance of the moment for both Leanne and the child. In many respects, this specific reflection marked a light-bulb moment within our focus group as it further prompted reflection upon their effect upon children's learning and development and upon themselves. As Tina says:

> My journey has been stressful – life changing. It has shaken up everything I do, not just my practice, which has changed, but personally. It's given me confidence, I can see that now. (Tina, 26, EYS)

Point for reflection

It has been said that change is a process not an event.

- Can you see in the words of the practitioners a recognition that change is indeed a process?
- Do your thoughts also resonate with their apprehension and concern that change has to be purposeful?
- To change and gain meaningful qualifications takes time, commitment and energy. Can you see yourself engaging in continuous professional development over time?
- Are you able to see how if you do so, you too will need to be part of this model of a community of practice?

Summary

There was an emphasis upon feeling valued as an overriding theme within our research. Not only as it reflected participants' understanding of the importance of their work as practitioners, but also in terms of the impact that the research process had upon them. Each described how it made them appreciate the importance of 'reflecting on what you have learned' and also of 'listening'. These final extracts sum this up:

> Being part of this research group has made me take stock. It's made me say things out loud. Hearing others and their experiences helps – actually sharing your experiences in such detail with others really brings it alive for you. (Lisa, 29, EYS)

> Talking about where I started and where I am now, listening to this group. Well I can't quite believe how much I have changed. (Sam, 31, EYS)

Analysis of the 'light-bulb' moments signal key points within learning journeys when learning 'fits into place'. These moments, as well as

(Continued)

(Continued)

learning incidences, were used to demonstrate the key aspects within each learning journey and indicate the importance of reflection. Our research process is central here and is acknowledged by all participants as providing them with the opportunity to reflect and articulate their experiences of the 'distance learning experience'. The importance of listening became a significant theme which we hope here demonstrates its own intrinsic value for practitioners in working together and with children and parents. The research allowed us to explore how a community of practice is potentially established, by providing opportunities for students to engage and reflect. Further, the students' learning journeys demonstrate the process of learning, as we see how they have moved from a novice, to returner into education, and on to a full group member. A model of a community of practice has proved useful in accommodating exploration of informal learning and so shedding light on the impact of reflection, collaboration and social interaction upon development, and how this can evoke a changing sense of self. Finally, we hope that this chapter indicates something of the importance of listening, sharing and collaboration both within a learning and practice setting.

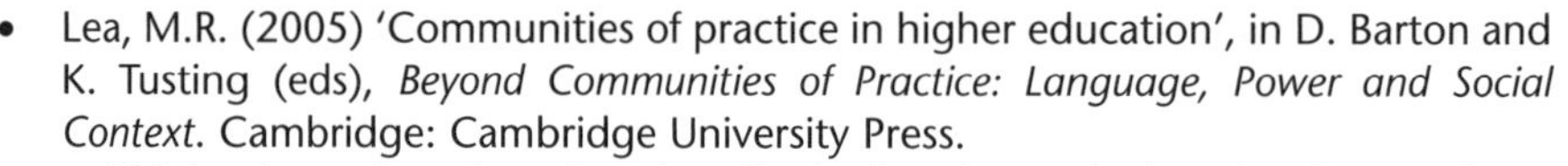

Suggested further reading

- Lea, M.R. (2005) 'Communities of practice in higher education', in D. Barton and K. Tusting (eds), *Beyond Communities of Practice: Language, Power and Social Context*. Cambridge: Cambridge University Press.

  This book consists of a series of studies by linguists and educational researchers, examining aspects of communities of practice. Theories of language-in-use, literacy practices, and discourse extend the concept and focus on issues around conflict, power, and the significance of the broader social context.

- Wenger, E. (1998) *Communities of Practice: Learning, Meaning and Identity*. Cambridge: Cambridge University Press.

  This book explores the idea that learning involves participation within a community of practice. The theory and practice of such communities are discussed, raising issues for educators and those concerned with lifelong learning.

- Wesley, P.W. and Buysse, V. (2001) 'Communities of practice: expanding professional roles to promote reflection and shared inquiry', *Topics in Early Childhood Special Education*, 21(2): 114–23.

  This article takes a practical approach and presents the skills needed to function as an effective consultant to educators and caregivers of children from birth to 5 years. A step-by-step model is introduced to demonstrate how interventions for young children with disabilities are more effective when the adults involved form collaborative partnerships.

References

Allard, C.C., Goldblatt, F.P., Kemball, I.J., Kendrick, S.A., Millen, K., Smith, J. and Deirdre, M. (2007) 'Becoming a reflective community of practice', *Reflective Practice Journal*, 8(3): 299–314.

Bolton, G. (2006) 'Narrative writing: reflective enquiry into professional practice', *Educational Action Research*, 14(2): 203–18.

Bruner, J. (1990) *Acts of Meaning*. Cambridge, MA: Harvard University Press.

Geertz, C. (1973) *The Interpretation of Culture*. New York: Basic Books.

Horowitz, C.R., Suchman, A.L., Branch, W.T. and Frankel, R.M. (2003) 'What do doctors find meaningful about their work?', *Annals of Internal Medicine*, 138(9): 772–6.

Hustler, D., McNamara, O., Jarvis, J., Londra, M., Campbell, A. and Howson, J. (2003) *Teachers Perceptions of Continuing Professional Development: DfES Research Report. RR429*. London: DfES.

Lave, J. and Wenger, E. (1991) *Situated Learning*. Cambridge: Cambridge University Press.

Lea, M.R. (2005) 'Communities of practice in higher education', in D. Barton and K. Tusting (eds), *Beyond Communities of Practice: Language, Power and Social Context*. Cambridge: Cambridge University Press.

Palincsar, A.S., Magnusson, S.J., Marano, N., Ford, D. and Brown, N. (1998) 'Designing a community of practice: principles and practices of the GlsML Community', *Teaching and Teacher Education*, 14(1): 5–19.

Robson, S. (2008) 'Supporting children's thinking in the Foundation Stage: practitioners' views on the role of initial training and continuing professional development', *Journal of In-Service Education*, 32(3): 341–57.

Rogers, J. (2000) 'Communities of practice: a framework for fostering coherence in virtual learning communities', *Educational Technology and Society*, 3(3): 384–92.

Siraj-Blatchford, I., Taggart, B., Sylva, K., Sammons, P. and Melhuish, E. (2008) 'Towards the transformation of practice in early childhood education: the Effective Provision of Pre-School Education (EPPE) Project', *Cambridge Journal of Education*, 38(1): 23–36.

Thomas, J. (1993) *Doing Critical Ethnography: Qualitative Research Methods*. Series 26. Los Angeles, CA, London and New Delhi: Sage Publications.

Wenger, E. (1998) *Communities of Practice: Learning, Meaning and Identity*. Cambridge: Cambridge University Press.

Wesley, P.W. and Buysse, V. (2001) 'Communities of practice: expanding professional roles to promote reflection and shared inquiry', *Topics in Early Childhood Special Education*, 21(2): 114–23.

11

Early Years Professionals: Leading for Change

Rory McDowall Clark and Sue Baylis

Chapter objectives

This chapter will examine the role of the Early Years Professional (EYP) and explore their contribution to quality provision for young children. The need for skilled and experienced graduates to lead practice was first identified in the Rumbold Report (DES, 1990) and endorsed by the findings of the Royal Society of Arts in their document Start Right: the Importance of Early Learning (Ball, 1994). More recently evidence from the Effective Provision of Pre-school Education (EPPE) project (Sylva et al., 2004) confirmed that trained graduates make a difference to meeting outcomes for young children. This expectation is now formalised in policy documents and legislation such as the 10-year childcare strategy, *Choice for Parents, the Best Start for Children* (HM Treasury, 2004) and the Childcare Act 2006. Early Years Professional Status (EYPS) is an important step in the professionalising of the early years workforce and demonstrates official recognition that '[the] single biggest factor that determines the quality of childcare is the workforce' (HM Treasury, 2004: 44). The skilled professionals to support such quality provision need opportunities for personal development and reflection in order to rise to such a challenge.

Although there is a growing literature on leadership in the early years (Aubrey, 2007; Callan and Robins, 2008; Rodd, 2006; Siraj-Blatchford and Manni, 2007) there has been little time as yet for analysis and evaluation of the new EYP role. Most would welcome initiatives that raise the profile of early years practice, but the dangers that come with increased regulation must also be recognised. Dahlberg and Moss (2005) remind us that prescribed frameworks for practice can be a way of governing the early years workforce and ensuring practitioners conform to approved norms. Concerns have also been raised that this 'regulatory gaze' can pressurise practitioners to adhere to a particular construction of professionalism (Osgood, 2006). The challenges and opportunities of the EYP role need to be set within this context.

Key questions raised in this chapter are:

- What is an Early Years Professional?
- What does an EYP do?
- How does an EYP lead practice?
- What learning can we take from these pictures of practice?

Early Years Professional Status supports the professional development of practitioners and provides formal recognition for their work in leading practice across the Early Years Foundation Stage. Their role is described in the EYPS candidate handbook in the following terms:

> Early Years Professionals will be key to raising the quality of early years provision. They will be change agents to improve practice. They will be expected to lead practice across the EYFS in a range of settings, modelling the skills and behaviours that promote good outcomes for children and supporting and mentoring other practitioners. (CWDC, 2007: 4)

Early Years Professional Status is a still a relatively recent initiative and the first people encouraged to attain this status were those who already had relevant qualifications. However the Government commitment to professionalising the workforce is evident in the aim to have EYPs in all children's centres by 2010 and in every full day-care setting by 2015. This has implications for all those presently working within the early years field or hoping to make this their career.

Although it is important to recognise the 'cultural, historical and political specificity ... of professionalism in relation to early childhood' (Osgood, 2006: 5), that does not prevent it from being a useful concept that is worthy of examination. Seeking to recognise specific characteristics that distinguish a profession from a job or occupation, Fromberg (1997) identified five specific features of professionalism:

- aspects of training;
- specialised knowledge;
- ethical practice;
- autonomy;
- control of entry into the field;
- existence of professional bodies.

Each of these can help us to explore the role of the EYP and will be referred to at different points within this chapter. In relation to becoming an EYP, aspects of training and control of entry into the field are key features intended to monitor the calibre of those aspiring to take on this role.

Recognition of the importance of graduate skills is evident in the expectation that those wishing to become EYPs should hold a degree and there are various routes to EYPS according to candidates' qualifications and experience. Those who already have a degree and relevant experience can go forward immediately for validation and there are alternative pathways for others who might lack experience across the full age range of the Early Years Foundation Stage or still be working towards graduate status (that is, hold a level 5 qualification such as a Foundation degree or HND). There is also a full-time pathway designed for graduates from other fields attracted to a career in early childhood, working in a similar way to PGCE (Postgraduate Certificate of Education) for those joining the teaching profession. Undergraduate routes for applicants with level 3 qualifications are currently being developed so in the future the normal expectation should be that those working with the under-5s have a graduate qualification. This will bring the UK in line with many other European countries (David, 1998;

Moss, 2006) but brings challenges in terms of appropriate opportunities to develop the complex interpersonal skills required to support such roles.

That professionalism requires more than knowledge alone is recognised by Fromberg (1997), who points out control of entry to the profession is also necessary. To be awarded Early Years Professional Status candidates must demonstrate how they meet 39 professional standards through a rigorous process including a number of written tasks and a full-day visit from a recognised assessor.

What does an EYP do?

Early Years Professionals are key to raising the quality of early years provision as agents of change and improving and promoting good outcomes for children. Their role is to lead practice across the Early Years Foundation Stage, supporting and mentoring other practitioners by modelling skills and behaviour. Early Years Professional Standard 24 specifically requires candidates to demonstrate how they are accountable for the delivery of high-quality provision (CWDC, 2007), showing recognition of the need for all professionals to take an active role in promoting quality. A leadership role is not necessarily the same thing as being 'in charge', although in smaller settings the EYP may also be the manager. (See Whalley, 2008, for a useful discussion of the difference between leading organisations and leading practice.) Many EYPs do not have a management role but lead from within a team – we shall consider some examples in the next two sections of this chapter.

One of the attributes that distinguishes a professional is autonomy (Fromberg, 1997) – the ability to determine your own actions and make independent decisions. This is important if practitioners are accountable for high-quality provision – simply following procedures because that is the way it has always been done does nothing to challenge poor practice and ensures it continues to exist. Margy Whalley's useful concept of 'constructive discontent' (2006) should underpin the role of EYPs in constantly questioning and challenging practice in order to improve provision. This is specifically identified in Standard 39 – 'Take a creative and constructively critical approach towards innovation, and adopt practice if benefits and improvements are identified' (CWDC, 2007).

Point for reflection

- Consider how autonomous you are in your work with children. What skills, knowledge and attributes does an EYP need in order to be properly autonomous?
- It has been suggested (Miller, 2008; Moss, 2006) that there is a danger that externally prescribed standards can inhibit professional autonomy and promote a model of technical practice. How can potential EYP candidates balance the various demands on their role to develop a sense of professional identity?

How does an EYP lead practice?

Every setting is different. We shall consider some pictures of practice here to demonstrate ways in which EYPs have developed and modelled good practice within a variety of contexts. All of the pictures of practice have had their personal details changed to provide anonymity and each of the following examples relates to Standard 3:

> candidates for EYPS should demonstrate through their practice knowledge and understanding of how children's well-being, development, learning and behaviour can be affected by a range of influences and transitions from inside and outside the setting. (CWDC, 2007: 24)

A picture of practice – Kerry

Kerry works in a large, well-established Children's Centre in an industrial town in the West Midlands. The clientele include a large number of Punjabi families some of whom have limited skills in written English. Kerry was concerned that children's transition to school was not managed as well as it might be and has worked hard to develop good partnerships with the local primary school to support this. However, a number of children whose parents are unfamiliar with the British school system worried about preparing their children for the next step. Kerry developed a 'Going to School Bag' containing items such as a school uniform, a lunchbox, a book of photographs of the school and Billy Bear dressed in his school uniform. This bag forms the basis of circle time discussions and children can take it home in a similar way to story sacks. In this way both children's and parents' anxieties can be addressed and children are prepared for a smooth transition.

A picture of practice – Teresa

Teresa is the Foundation Stage Coordinator in a private day nursery in an old church hall. Like Kerry she has thought carefully about preparing children who are leaving nursery to begin school and the nursery has developed a special celebration for children and parents. The older children moving on are congratulated and staff prepare individual memory boards for them commemorating special things they achieved at nursery. One little boy lost his father in a road accident during his last year at nursery and Teresa supported both him and his mother through this difficult time. She made sure that the reception class teacher was aware of his circumstances but also realised that the leaving ceremony, as a family celebration, would inevitably make both mother and child very aware of the absence of his father. Arrangements were made to borrow a large bubble machine to set up in the garden alongside the children and parents. Teresa explained to the boy that Daddy would have liked to have been there to hear all about his special memories at nursery but that the bubbles would blow away into the air taking all their thoughts to him. Not only did this thoughtful provision make the transition much easier for the child but his mother also appreciated Teresa's sensitivity.

A picture of practice – Becky

At the time of her EYP assessment Becky was room leader in a large private day nursery working with 3-year-olds. Children of this age often find it difficult to articulate their feelings and Becky introduced Stripy the tiger, a stuffed toy animal, to circle time to support their emotional development. Stripy 'lived' in a particular place in the room so children knew how to find him any time they might want to cuddle up on Becky's lap and have a chat with Stripy. On one occasion a little girl's house was burgled and she became very nervous about going to bed, frightened to sleep in case the burglars should return. Stripy went home with the little girl and slept in her bed to look after her until she got over her fear and began to feel safe again.

Point for reflection

- Young children undergo a number of changes we can predict, such as moving on to another part of the nursery or beginning school. What have you seen that you would identify as good practice to support these transitions? The EYFS practice guidance states that 'transition should be seen as a process and not an event' (DCSF, 2008: 10). Are you confident this is true of practice in your own setting?

(Continued)

(Continued)

- The EYFS practice guidance suggests 'settings should communicate information which will secure continuity of experience for children between settings' (DCSF, 2008: 10). Is information sufficient? Think about the sensitive ways Kerry and Teresa supported children's continuity of experience. What specific features of your setting should you take into account to ensure smooth transitions?
- Individual children also undergo transitions in their lives outside the setting which affect their well-being; examples are the birth of new siblings or family breakdown. What strategies do you have in place to support both children's anticipated and unexpected experiences?
- Who else was involved in the three examples outlined above? How have each of these professionals been able to model and share good practice?
- How can an EYP demonstrate leadership and support of others in their everyday practice?

A particular feature of the professional is that they hold specialised knowledge (Fromberg, 1997) and that this is used to inform their practice. All EYPs have studied at graduate level but this knowledge needs to be practically applied in their everyday work with children. This relates to Simkins' (2005) concept of knowledge-in-practice, raised in Chapter 1 by Karen Appleby. Another two examples will illustrate this:

A picture of practice – Kerry

The Children's Centre where Kerry works is purpose built with constant access to a well-planned outdoor area. Children had become very interested in making 'potions', so a range of pots and pans, plastic bottles, wooden spoons and powdered colours were provided for them to explore and experiment with. As part of building work a lorry-load of gravel was delivered but due to access problems this needed to be dumped at the gateway. The children used wheelbarrows and trucks to transport the gravel to its final site. A number of them began wrapping pieces of gravel in coloured paper to make 'sweets'. Kerry supported the children with resources to develop their own shop, later organising a visit to an old-fashioned sweet shop where they could see sweets being weighed out of big jars.

A picture of practice – Penny

Penny runs a pre-school in a village hall. Many other community groups use the hall and all equipment and resources need to be stored away at the end of sessions. Despite these restrictions Penny still manages to ensure there are plenty of opportunities for stimulating child-led activities. Following the story of The Three Billy Goats Gruff children became very interested in re-enacting the story. Play developed over several days with children progressing from making small bridges with construction to creating bridges they themselves could use over a river assembled from a complex array of drainpipes and guttering.

Point for reflection

- Kerry and Penny work in very different circumstances. In what ways do their approaches both demonstrate good practice in play and learning? Consider the discussion of play in Chapter 2 by Natalie Canning.
- How have they established effective outdoor learning environments? How does this connect with the EYFS theme of 'enabling environments'? (DCSF, 2008). Think about your own setting – are there ways in which you can make better use of the environment and thereby extend opportunities and experiences for the children?
- If you are familiar with the EYPS standards see how many standards you can match to these examples. In particular link them to the standards for effective practice.

The broader picture

The role of the EYP has been developed in relation to the Early Years Foundation Stage (DCSF, 2008) which became statutory in England in September 2008. Early Years Professionals are viewed as vital to the successful implementation of the EYFS and so there is a strong correlation between EYPS standards and the principles underpinning the EYFS. The examples considered so far all centre on the child although the role of others is implicit, but children's lives take place within a broad environmental context (Bronfenbrenner, 1979) and practitioners need to operate beyond the confines of the setting itself.

The most important relationship is obviously with parents and carers. The EYFS Principles into Practice state:

> Parents are children's first and most enduring educators. When parents and practitioners work together in early years settings, the results have a positive impact on children's development and learning. (DCSF, 2008: Positive Relationships 2.2)

Such an expectation envisages more than simply sharing information with parents at the beginning and end of the day and requires a positive proactive approach. The following are all examples of how EYPs have actively worked in partnership with parents to improve outcomes for their children.

A picture of practice – Juliet

Part of Juliet's role in a Children's Centre involved outreach work with families. Keen to encourage parents' and carers' confidence in interacting with their children and developing their communication skills, she developed a song workshop which parents and children attended together. Over a period of several weeks parents increased their repertoire of songs which they could continue with their children at home. At the end of the project a CD of the songs was produced for everyone to keep.

A picture of practice – Helen

Helen also used music to encourage parental partnership in working together for children. As a full-time EYP candidate in a Children's Centre she developed a collection of song sacks which were available for use within the setting as well as for parents to take home and share with their children. Each song sack contained a CD along with laminated cards and a variety of related items to give parents confidence to engage with their children in activities that supported rhythm, sounds and music.

A picture of practice – Ruth

A very skilled practitioner with the over-3 age group, Ruth had had less experience with babies, so following the Short Extended Pathway to EYPS gave her the opportunity to develop this (CWDC, 2007). She spent time in the baby room at a Children's Centre where she developed a good

(Continued)

(Continued)

rapport with the parents. Ruth organised a workshop working alongside parents and helping them to identify each baby's unique development. She used large cardboard rolls from a carpet store with the crawling babies to encourage movement and exploration and involved parents in parachute play with their children. She encouraged 'listening' to the babies, supporting parents' confidence in their ability to recognise their child's particular interests and support their curiosity.

A picture of practice – Claire

Working with 'parents' more often than not in reality means working with mothers and it can be much more difficult to involve fathers in early years settings. Claire worked in a kindergarten where she wanted to encourage fathers to become more involved with their children's learning. She organised a MAK (Men and Kids) club, a lunchtime 'Stay and Play' opportunity for both dads and granddads with support in place for single parents.

A picture of practice – Heather

Heather also thought creatively about a range of strategies to encourage fathers into the nursery where she worked. As most men were working during the week she planned for alternative times and arranged curry nights and a Saturday morning dad's group.

Point for reflection

- How does your setting show that it truly values and respects parents' contribution to children's development, learning and well-being?
- What strategies do you have to develop partnerships with parents to support children's learning and development?
- How could you develop your partnership with parents more?

Beyond the microsystem of the child's life within the family and setting there is a range of connections within the mesosystem (Bronfenbrenner, 1979) which also impact on their well-being. The way in which an EYP's role interfaces with other settings and organisations depends on a variety of factors, including type of setting, geographical area, local authority organisation and the particular circumstances of families. All this is explicit in EYPS Standards 6, 23 and 36:

> **S6** The contribution that other professionals within the setting and beyond can make to children's physical and emotional well-being, development and learning.
>
> **S23** Identify and support children whose progress, development or well-being is affected by changes or difficulties in their personal circumstances and know when to refer them to colleagues for specialist support.
>
> **S36** Contribute to the work of a multi-professional team and where appropriate, co-ordinate and implement agreed programmes and interventions on a day-to-day basis. (CWDC, 2007: 24)

The following are just a few examples of ways in which these standards are apparent through the ways that EYPs take a multi-professional and multi-agency approach in their work with children:

- acting as SENCO (Special Educational Needs Coordinator) and/or liaising with the Area SENCO to support children in the setting;
- contributing observations and assessments for an Educational Psychologist;
- attending case conferences or supporting parents in doing this;
- involvement in the development of Individual Education Plans (IEPs);
- implementing a particular programme of support in conjunction with a Speech and Language Therapist;
- developing a support group for parents with a Health Visitor;
- liaising with Social Workers and preparing reports for court cases and official hearings;
- developing partnerships with local community groups;
- taking part in a variety of local forums and early years groups.

Some EYPs will be working in roles where liaison with others is the major part of their role – for instance a Speech and Language specialist with a children's charity whose peripatetic role supported staff in several nurseries or Early Years Advisory Teachers. However the majority of EYPs are based in one setting where they maintain and develop good practice with a specific clientele of children and families.

Point for reflection

- Make a list of everyone you come into contact with over the course of your job. Were you surprised at how many people this includes? How clear are you about their roles and responsibilities? Are you confident of the circumstances in which you would contact them and how you would go about this?
- The EYFS expects all practitioners to work in partnership with other professionals to help children meet the outcomes of *Every Child Matters* – how confident are you of your familiarity with this and other important legislation and policies?
- How can you extend and increase your involvement with other professionals and organisations to improve outcomes for the young children in your care?
- Should the role of the EYP be to encourage, to develop or to build on the skills of others?

The importance of ethical practice, another feature of professionalism (Fromberg, 1997), is evident in these issues. As well as their work with children, an EYP's need to liaise between parents, children, organisations and other professionals from a wide range of backgrounds brings with it serious responsibilities. It is essential they are able to respond to a range of complex situations in an appropriate manner. It is necessary to develop relationships with families that tread the fine line between friendship and professional objectivity and to respect individuals' differing opinions whilst still maintaining a principled stance. Awareness of appropriate boundaries, the ability to resolve conflicts, balance responsibilities and obligations, respect confidentiality, whilst also considering where priorities might demand sharing of information and the capacity to deal with divergence of values, are all aspects of this.

What learning can we take from these pictures of practice?

The Statutory Framework for the EYFS begins with the statement:

> Every child deserves the best possible start in life and support to fulfil their potential. A child's experience in the early years has a major impact on their future life chances. A secure, safe and happy childhood is important in its own right, and it provides the foundation for children to make the most of their abilities and talents as they grow up. (DCSF, 2008: 7)

If you are reading this book it is fair to assume you are already committed to this viewpoint, which carries the implicit necessity for highly qualified and creative people to develop such provision. Early Years Professional Status is part of a national commitment to ensure a world-class workforce, and the first EYPs are already having an impact on practice.

Early Years Professionals are expected not only to model good practice themselves but also 'to lead and support others' (CWDC, 2007: 24). It is evident from the examples shown as pictures of practice within this chapter that leadership of this sort can be envisioned as something distinct from a managerial or supervisory role. A considerable number of EYPs successfully influence practice from *within* their teams, having an impact on provision through their willingness to evaluate and innovate. In this way the impact is wide, affecting the practice of others like ripples in a pond. Acting as agents of change, EYPs encourage colleagues to engage in continuing professional development and support a culture of lifelong learning within their settings. A number of EYPs act in a mentor role supporting others to gain the status.

One thing common to all is the benefit derived from the opportunity for reflection and learning. The graduate status of EYPs recognises the need for reflective practitioners but actually undertaking the process of assessment and validation requires practitioners to stop and really examine their practice through a critical lens. Discussing and sharing ideas with others from across a wide range of different settings and local authorities is stimulating and creates increased levels of confidence in leading practice. A number of EYPs have received outstanding Ofsted reports which they attribute to undertaking EYPS. This is not because they were not already excellent practitioners but because the route to EYPS helped make them more self-aware and conscious of their own practice. As a result they are able to analyse, evaluate and justify what they do and ensure their approach to planning focuses on the child's interests and needs – to deliver the 'personalised learning, development and care' which 'lies at the heart of the EYFS' (DCSF, 2008: 6).

To continue the analogy of ripples, the impact of EYPs continues to spread. An important element of this is networking and there are many ways in which EYPs continue to share practice and support each other, building on new friendships and contacts. Some local authorities have set up networks of EYPs to lead new developments and there are also Internet forums where dialogue takes place across wider geographical boundaries. Thus practitioners are able to engage in the exchange of ideas in such a way that confirms and endorses the recognition of specialised skilled experts as a profession. The final aspect of Fromberg's (1997) analysis of professionalism is the existence of professional bodies. Historically the fragmented nature of early years provision meant that there was no concerted voice to speak for practitioners in the field. Recently the Association of Professionals in Education and Children's Trusts (Aspect) has developed a national committee of EYPs to lobby for an appropriate national pay framework and recognised career progression. This is particularly important as one of the major concerns about the viability of this lead professional role is levels of pay and status in comparison with qualified teachers. The affordability of the new workforce is one of the greatest challenges facing the sector in the future (Miller, 2008; Moss, 2006).

Such a profound change in the landscape has not been without problems. The role of the early years worker was for many years viewed as unskilled 'women's work' and new expectations may be unsettling for some who felt comfortable within such roles. For instance resentment can arise when practitioners who have been in their job for many years feel they might be displaced by newly qualified graduates with relatively limited experience. Miller and Cable (2008), in their exploration of the role of the professional within the early years workforce, offer valuable insights into the challenges this presents.

Summary

The last decade has seen huge changes in the field of early years; for those of us working in this area for many years, this is long overdue, but no less welcome for that. Those new to the profession join it at an exciting time when the years before statutory education are no longer viewed as less important than what follows, but as the foundation of all future learning. The creation of a new category of professionals, the Early Years Professionals, as specialised experts working with children up to five is fundamental to this change.

Suggested further reading

- Miller, L. and Cable, C. (eds) (2008) *Professionalism in the Early Years.* London: Hodder Arnold.

  An important consideration of the challenges and possibilities raised by the drive for professionalism in the early years sector.

- Whalley, M.E. (2008) *Leading Practice in Early Years Settings*. Exeter: Learning Matters.
  A very useful guide to good practice to support those hoping to attain EYPS. Many case studies and examples help to illustrate professional standards in practice.

- Wild, M. and Mitchell, H. (2007) *Early Childhood Studies: A Reflective Reader*. Exeter: Learning Matters.
  This book includes chapters about a range of relevant topics such as multi-professional working, listening to children and the role of policy makers.

Useful websites for resources mentioned in this chapter

The Children's Workforce Development Council was set up to support the children's workforce across England to implement Every Child Matters: www.cwdccouncil.org.uk

The EYPS forum is an interactive site which supports EYPs and EYPS candidates:
www.eyps.info/

Association of Professionals in Education and Children's Trusts (Aspect): www.aspect.org.uk
A professional organisation serving practitioners working in the early years sector. The organisation lobbies for recognition and improved conditions.

References

Aubrey, C. (2007) *Leading and Managing in the Early Years*. London: Sage Publications.
Ball, C. (1994) *Start Right: The Importance of Early Learning*. London: Royal Society for Arts.
Bronfenbrenner, U. (1979) *The Ecology of Human Development*. Cambridge, MA: Harvard University Press.
Callan, S. and Robins, A. (2008) *Managing and Leading in the Early Years*. London: Sage Publications.
Children's Workforce Development Council (CWDC) (2007) *Candidates Handbook: a Guide to the Gateway Review and Assessment Process*. London: CWDC.
Dahlberg, G. and Moss, P. (2005) *Ethics and Politics in Early Childhood Education*. London: Routledge Falmer.
David, T. (ed.) (1998) *Researching Early Childhood Education: European Perspectives*. London: Paul Chapman Publishing.
Department for Children, Schools and Families (DCSF) (2008) *Practice Guidance for the Early Years Foundation Stage*. Nottingham: DCSF.

Department of Education and Science (DES) (1990) *Starting with Quality: Report of the Committee of Enquiry into the Quality of Educational Experience Offered to Three and Four Year Olds*. Rumbold Report. London: HMSO.

Fromberg, D. (1997) 'The professional status of early childhood educators', in J. Isenberg and M.R.C. Jalongo (eds), *The Professional and Social Status of the Early Childhood Educator: Challenges, Controversies and Insights*. New York: Columbia Teachers College Press.

Her Majesty's (HM) Treasury (2004) *Choice for Parents, the Best Start for Children: A 10 Year Strategy for Childcare*. London: HM Treasury.

Miller, L. (2008) 'Developing professionalism within a regulatory framework in England: challenges and possibilities', *European Early Childhood Education Research Journal*, 16(2): 255–68.

Miller, L. and Cable, C. (eds) (2008) *Professionalism in the Early Years*. London: Hodder Arnold.

Moss, P. (2006) 'Structures, understandings and discourses: possibilities for re-envisioning the early childhood worker', *Contemporary Issues in Early Childhood*, 7(1): 30–41.

Osgood, J. (2006) 'Deconstructing professionalism in early childhood education: resisting the regulatory gaze', *Contemporary Issues in Early Childhood*, 7(1): 5–14.

Rodd, J. (2006) *Leadership in Early Childhood*, 3rd edn. Maidenhead: Open University Press.

Simkins, T. (2005) 'Leadership in Education: "What Works" or "What Makes Sense"?' *Educational Management, Administration and Leadership*, 33(1): 9–26.

Siraj-Blatchford, I. and Manni, L. (2007) *Effective Leadership in the Early Years Sector: The ELEYS Study*. London: Institute of Education, University of London.

Sylva, K., Melhuish, E.C., Sammons, P., Siraj-Blatchford, I. and Taggart, B. (2004) *The Effective Provision of Pre-School Education (EPPE) Project: Final Report*. London: DfEE/Institute of Education, University of London.

Whalley, M. (2006) 'Children's centres: the new frontier for the welfare state and the education system? [online] www.ncsl.org.uk/media/-56a-36-childrens-centres-whalley.pdf (accessed 04.11.2008).

Whalley, M.E. (2008) *Leading Practice in Early Years Settings*. Exeter: Learning Matters.

12

Defining and Measuring Quality in Early Years Settings

Alison Jackson

Chapter objectives

The following chapter offers reflection upon definitions and measurements of 'quality' early years provision from a range of perspectives including aspects of social, cultural and historical viewpoints. It is concerned with the way practitioners might improve outcomes for children but specifically seeks to listen to the voice of a key stakeholder group in early years provision, namely, parents. I believe this to be important because throughout my professional development I have been encouraged to look at working in partnership with parents but this has tended to be providing information about quality prescribed by the Government. It has rarely involved parents making their own views known regarding aspects of quality provision they actually seek. Therefore this chapter considers the differing values attributed to defining quality as perceived by parents and practitioners. In this way it becomes possible to listen to stakeholders 'voices', leading to a deeper understanding of their views and to then reflect upon quality as part of a practitioner's role, their key responsibilities and the importance of forging positive relationships with parents. My views are based upon my experience over the last 20 years in a variety of early years settings. This has involved supervising pre-school groups, childminding and being an active participant in committee working.

With the advent of new curriculum frameworks emerging in all of the four nations of the UK, the timing and focus of this chapter is apt. All four nations advocate building positive and collaborative working relationships with parents. Many local authorities are also considering parental views on quality, with 'quality of childcare' being cited by 75 per cent of respondents in a recent Childcare Assessment Report as being the factor that most influenced their (parents) choice of childcare (Herefordshire County Council Early Years Extended Services, 2007).

Point for reflection

Having introduced the idea of viewing quality from the perspective of a parent we can ask the following questions:

- Who defines quality?
- How can it be measured?
- What is it in practice?
- Do parents and practitioners have the same perception and/or understanding of quality?

Who defines quality? A historical perspective

Pioneers including Montessori, Froebel and MacMillan advocated the value of nursery education as a means of promoting child development in the early 20th century. However, historically society and the public policy agenda, held the view that young children should be at home with their mothers. This meant that there was little provision or resources for any form of childcare, and quality issues were perceived not to be significant. This did not change until the 1967 Plowden Report, which included nursery education in the Government review of primary education. This recommended only the provision of part-time sessions, arguably due to the high cost incurred in providing full-time quality services rather than the claim at the time that young children would not be able to cope being away from their mothers for whole days (Flett, 2008).

In the ensuing 30 years that passed before the implementation of a policy for state nursery education, there was a huge growth in parent-managed voluntary playgroups. This could not cope with the demand for childcare provision as women took increasing opportunities for employment available to them, so market forces drove an expansion in private day-care centres and childminding services. These were all regulated by a framework defined by social services that focused on standards of care and adequacy of facilities only, although this was extended and underpinned by the Children Act 1989 (Baldock et al., 2005). As the quantity of early years provision increased and as Pugh (2006: 8) describes how 'fragmented and uncoordinated' early years services were at the end of the 20th century, there was a need to address issues of maintaining quality.

The Rumbold Report, *Starting with Quality* (DES, 1990), and the Royal Society of Arts Report, *Start Right* (Ball, 1994), both stressed the importance of quality in early years education. The Rumbold Committee (DES, 1990) made several recommendations that can still be recognised in best practice for early years settings today including:

- play having a fundamental role as a foundation for learning;
- the importance of collaborative working;
- and coordination of services.

Many researchers, authors and practitioners, share the view of the Rumbold Committee (DES, 1990) that care and education are inseparable in a quality curriculum (Abbott, 1994; Ball, 1994; Melhuish, 2003; Sylva et al., 2004). Ball (1994) recommended that high-quality provision be made available to all 3- and 4-year-olds, reviewing evidence that high-quality early education leads to lasting cognitive and social benefits in children and set out the following major prerequisites for 'high quality' provision:

- an appropriate early learning curriculum;
- the selection, training, and continuity of staff;
- high staff to children ratios;
- buildings and equipment designed for early learning;
- a partnership role for parents.

Baldock et al. (2005) and Flett (2008) claim that it was the social agenda to address child poverty by enabling parents to work rather than education benefits that drove the Labour Government (elected in 1997) to finally promise a free part-time nursery education place for every 3- and 4-year old. However, it may be argued that because the free entitlement currently only covers 12.5 hours and the employment threshold for receipt of working tax credit is 16 hours this does little to help people access employment. The proposed rise to 15 hours' free entitlement will only in part address this dilemma.

Towards a definition of quality?

Early Years practitioners in the 21st century are faced with many demands to provide a 'quality' service. Practitioners are bombarded by requirements to deliver a quality early years curriculum; to achieve quality assurance and to build a quality workforce. This drive for quality is the culmination of many years of research into effective practice and how to achieve the best outcomes for children but is also linked to social policy. Social policy is a statement of a government's intent to take action to improve the welfare of its citizens and is developed within the historical, social and cultural contexts that exist at any point in time (Baldock et al., 2005). The concept of quality will therefore be different in other societies and cultures where the political, legal and economic systems that encompass attitudes and values of that society will determine the quality of childcare provided.

Moss (1994: 1) explains how the definition of quality in early childhood services will reflect the 'values and beliefs, needs and agendas, influence and empowerment of various "stakeholder" groups' and so the concept will be subjective and relative rather than an objective reality. Any definition of quality will therefore not only be complex but will also depend on whose views are included and what measures are used (Mooney et al., 2003; Moss, 1994; Woodhead, 1996). This also means that the definition of quality will change and vary over time to take account of the different contexts of provision for young children and the sector involved. Flett (2008) states that historically, in the United Kingdom, these have included health, childcare, education and community development. Both Moss (1994) and Flett (2008) claim that as the beliefs and values of society change, so will the definition of quality of both provision and the regulatory framework, due to the influence of social forces upon research, policy and practice in early years.

How is quality measured?

Currently, the Government uses minimum, measurable welfare requirements for state registration and inspection of early years settings that include:

- safe and healthy environments;
- management of behaviour;
- suitably trained and qualified staff with associated minimum supervision levels;
- adult/child ratios;
- safe, suitable and well-maintained equipment, furniture and space both inside and out;
- a well-planned and resourced, stimulating and challenging curriculum, tailored to each individual child's needs and appropriately maintained records to efficiently manage the setting and meet the needs of the children (DCSF, 2008).

These are now integrated with the curriculum learning and development requirements of the Early Years Foundation Stage (EYFS) in England that claim to improve the quality and consistency of childcare from birth to 5, enabling parents to be assured that, no matter which setting they access for their child, 'essential standards of provision are in place' (DCSF, 2008: 10).

Under the Childcare Act 2006, these are inspected by the Office for Standards in Education (Ofsted) and parents have access to the published inspection reports (DCSF, 2008). There are critics of this new curriculum but I can only offer support for their concerns about the interpretation of the EYFS rather than the content. I agree with Flett's (2008) views of resources being the real issue hidden behind concepts of quality and that providing a quality curriculum will not provide a quality service unless the workforce is of equal quality to deliver it. Kazimirski et al. (2008) and the Government's statutory guidance, *Raising Standards – Improving Outcomes* (DCSF, 2006), supports and extends this view by proposing that ongoing sustainable quality improvement cannot occur without strong management and leadership.

The National Children's Bureau was appointed as lead body to develop a National Quality Improvement Network (NQIN, 2007) whose role is to help local authorities drive quality improvement through a set of good practice principles in early years services and so improve outcomes as identified in *Every Child Matters* (DfES, 2004). *Raising Standards – Improving Outcomes* (DCSF, 2006) was intended to link with other quality improvement initiatives and support delivery of the EYFS, underpinned by the Children Act 2004 and Childcare Act 2006. Fawcett (2000) and the NQIN (2007) both propose that to evaluate the quality of a child's daily experience in a preschool setting, it is necessary to look at other measures such as the ten-point framework of the Effective Early Learning (EEL) project (Pascal and Bertram, 1997), that include 'child involvement' and 'adult engagement', as well as the curriculum framework.

This view is supported by Moss (1994: 2), who claims that to evaluate quality many researchers have turned to indirect measures using elements of service such as 'child–adult interactions' and factors such as 'staff ratios and training'. These measures, usually determined by researchers and other experts, can then be used to set targets or goals for settings to work towards but these may not be the same goals of other interested stakeholders such as parents or children. Katz (1994) and Brophy and Statham (1994) propose that these 'top down' measures of quality actually constrict the concept of quality and they should be used in combination with a 'bottom up' approach. This would include the quality of the experiences that children, parents and staff have in relation to the early years provision and how childcare serves both the community and society at large.

Although quality is a requirement that is constantly being evaluated, it is often not fully implemented due to lack of financial and technical support (Peralta, 2008). This must be addressed and to do this the voices of not only the experts but also the parents, children and their communities must be taken into account. In Nordic countries and some parts of Italy, where the structural conditions for quality are already met, this has been taken to the extreme where children, parents, and staff decide and develop the quality objectives and the procedures for evaluating them (Mooney et al., 2003).

I have visited other childcare facilities that on first, indefinable impressions have impacted on me as being 'quality' settings but this is certainly not something measurable and I agree with Moss (1994: 2) that there is another analytical or descriptive meaning of quality that can be applied to early years regarding the nature, ethos and 'underlying dynamics of a particular service'. A view supported by Siraj-Blatchford and MacLeod-Brudenell (1999: 45) who note that, although it can be difficult to describe quality provision for young children generally, 'we can recognise it when we see it'.

Point for reflection

It may be useful here to consider 'quality' in terms of the ethos that pervades a setting. Every setting that encompasses care for young children communicates its own ethos and it can be argued that the environment exudes a perception of quality.

- How do you achieve this in your setting?
- How do parents know that they are welcome and that they will be listened to?
- How do you demonstrate that you work well with your colleagues?
- How do you communicate to parents how you support their child's learning and development, and personal, social and emotional well-being?

Parents may have preconceived ideas about a setting based on shared views with other parents, but they will still make up their own minds based on what they see and 'feel' when they enter a setting. Parents will notice if children are encouraged to ask questions, discuss ideas, develop materials, feel confident to try things out and make mistakes. In this way parents are constantly aware of the physical environment and how each setting presents its own ethos and visible mark of 'quality'.

The criteria for judging quality

A substantial amount of the research regarding quality, with an emphasis on the impact of childcare provision on the social, emotional and intellectual development of children, has been undertaken in the USA (Mooney et al., 2003). The Committee for Economic Development Report (CED, 1993) noted that most parents, when responding to surveys, usually indicated that quality was the most important factor they desired in childcare. However, the report suggests that parents use different criteria to professionals when judging quality. Mooney and Munton (1998) found that parents and childcare professionals often hold very different perspectives on certain 'quality' themes. Parents of very young children acknowledge the importance of the relationship between the caregiver and the child but are less concerned with the level of training of staff. As one parent states, 'you can't teach someone to love children' (Larner and Phillips, 1994: 52).

However, once their child is in pre-school, parents often then define quality of childcare as being dependent on the educational content (CED, 1993; Mooney and Munton, 1998). The CED report (1993) further claims that research has shown that many parents feel guilty about placing their child in an early years setting that is only deemed adequate by the professionals and, in these circumstances, they do not like discussing quality of childcare. Parental choice of setting was found to be based on affordability, availability and flexibility, rather than professional definitions of quality (CED, 1993; Larner and Phillips, 1994; Mooney and Munton, 1998).

With little consultation regarding parents' perspectives of quality of childcare, it has been left to early years professionals to define quality and inform policy-makers. Professionals assess childcare against measurable positive and effective outcomes and experiences for children. Initially the focus was on structural concepts that included ratios of adult/child, sizes of groups and practitioners' qualifications. Although these factors could promote good outcomes for children, Larner and Phillips (1994) and Ceglowski (2004) stated that they provided neither a direct measurement of quality nor guaranteed it.

One of the most comprehensive and influential studies in the UK that compounded the perspective of structural quality was the Effective Provision of Pre-School Education (EPPE) project (Sylva et al., 2004). This longitudinal study used measurements based on the standardised and revised 'Early Childhood Environment Rating Scale' (ECERS-R) (Harms et al., 1998) and a further 4-point scale based on curricular factors (ECERS-E) (Sylva et al., 2003). Brophy and Statham (1994) argue that the original scales were validated by the views of American experts specialising in Childhood and did not take account of the various other stakeholders involved, including parents. However, the revised scales appear to have taken into account some of the areas perceived as missing from the first scales, including parental involvement and interpersonal interaction. Additionally, the EPPE study and other reports did conclude that the relationships between adults and children in the settings were especially important and that warm, sensitive, responsive interactions added to the measured quality (NAO, 2004; Sylva et al., 2004).

The current recognised criteria for judging quality is about imposing adult views on children and professional views on parents (Woodhead, 1996). There is also the subjective nature of quality provision and practice. Quality is often something that you can't put your finger on, but know that it is there. Emlen et al. (2000, cited in Halle and Vick, 2007) attempted to measure parents' perceptions of quality childcare by evaluating specific descriptive characteristics rather than satisfaction. Key factors included:

- warmth and interest in my child;
- rich activities and environment;
- skilled caregiver through sharing information;
- child feels safe and secure.

In an attempt to raise the importance of quality for parents, Herefordshire Early Years Development and Childcare Partnership (EYDCP, 2008) offered suggestions for questions about quality that they should ask including:

- provision of information;
- how welcoming the setting is;
- interactions between staff and children and staff and parents;
- resources;
- safety on the premises.

However these indicators continue to support a structural and practical understanding of what quality is rather than centring on the experiences of the child. Just because a setting is well maintained, colourful and meets health and safety requirements, does not mean that it provides a quality experience for individual children.

Point for reflection

When parents talk about 'quality' are they referring to the concept as defined by researchers and other professionals in early years or their own view of what 'quality' means for them personally?

The Childcare and Early Years Survey 2007 (Kazimirski et al., 2008: 13) researched parents' use, views and experiences of Early Years Provision in England and stated that '63 per cent of parents rated the quality of local childcare services as very or fairly good'. However, this report did not attempt to offer any definition of quality but found the main reasons that parents chose formal childcare for their children were 'trust', the 'good reputation' of the setting, 'care combined with education' and a desire for their child to 'mix' with other children (Kazimirski et al., 2008: 121). East Dunbartonshire Council's parents' Early Years and Childcare Survey carried out in 2006 did provide indicators of quality that parents could use to gauge their response and 98 per cent of respondents specified they were happy with the high quality of care their child received and 94 per cent that the quality of the curriculum on offer was high. These are useful and worthwhile reports but raise the question as to how this view of quality was arrived at. Should we 'professionalise' our questions in such a way as to elicit a '*professional*' response from parents? On the other hand, should we give such little information about how to consider quality, that it gains a response that is impressionistic and not very constructive? Could the answer be to encourage reflection? Should we be asking 'why', 'what', 'how' and 'who' questions? In this way, we might aim to assimilate the views of others, share good practice, and try to understand differing values and beliefs. We might even start to co-construct solutions to problems, evaluate what we mean by quality, and celebrate success.

A picture of practice – what is quality in practice?

I conducted a small-scale study seeking the views of 100 parents and 20 practitioners. Questionnaires were distributed and participants were asked to comment on what they perceived quality childcare to be. The majority of practitioners felt that quality was a significant issue for parents when choosing childcare, but one practitioner also reflected:

(Continued)

(Continued)

> Our nursery is a feeder for the school, it is free and parents want their children to be with their peer group for school. They very rarely question what we offer. We volunteer information on why we do things. (Nursery Practitioner, October 2008)

A parent also commented that quality is difficult to define as it can be interpreted in different ways and it depends largely on individual choice and perception. It is also important that children are settled and happy to attend. Children should be at the centre of any quality processes, one parent reflected:

> Friends in the village took their children [to the setting] so my daughter knew the other children which made her relaxed and happy, which I feel is the most important thing. Happy children learn/play better in my opinion. (Parent, October 2008)

From the study parents felt that although they recognised the importance of their children being happy and settled, practicalities of childcare greatly influenced their choice, such as proximity to work and convenience for drop-off and pick-up times. In addition the overall factors selected by parents as main contributions to quality in early years settings were:

- children are well supervised;
- suitable staff CRB (Criminal Records Bureau) checks carried out and references obtained;
- emergency evacuation procedures in place;
- well trained and/or supervised staff;
- welcoming, friendly, enthusiastic staff;
- sensitive and caring interactions between adults and children;
- working in partnership with parents, for example, settling in, managing behaviour, sharing information.

In comparison practitioners viewed the top priorities for quality as:

- planning for individual child's learning and developmental needs;
- procedures/provision to support children with additional needs;
- well trained and/or supervised staff with opportunities to access further training;
- staff recognising the importance of a child's home as a learning environment;
- sensitive and caring interactions between adults and children;
- clear and consistent behaviour management;
- working in partnership with parents, for example, settling in, managing behaviour, sharing information;
- staff working as a team, modelling positive roles and relationships with shared aims and ethos.

(Continued)

(Continued)

Practical issues such as a clean and hygienic environment and high adult/child ratios appropriate to age and stage of the development of children also appeared on the practitioners' list; however, the striking difference between the two is how the child is at the centre of quality practice on the practitioners' top priorities list, whereas practical implications preoccupy parents' views.

Safety and security and the interactions between suitably trained staff, parents and the children in their care were seen as significant factors by most parents. All the practitioners recognised the same quality factors apart from having an emergency evacuation procedure in place. This does in fact raise some concerns as this is a legal requirement under the EYFS. However, the questionnaire was about 'quality' factors and the practitioners may have held the opinion that legal requirements do not necessarily enhance quality.

A statement included on the questionnaire asked respondents if they thought quality practice involved 'teaching children to read and write'. This view did not rate highly with the practitioners yet nearly half of the parents thought it was very important. Children's educational attainment appears to be an expectation by parents. However, happy children, experiencing fun and enjoyable activities were mentioned by several parents and one parent recognised that for this to happen the staff would also need to be happy, valued and motivated. One parent commented that training staff had no purpose if they did not have a natural empathy and love of children.

There was a lack of importance placed by parents on provision for supporting children with additional needs. However, this may be explained by the sample of parents not having any children with additional needs. For them personally this may not be an issue, as the term quality conjures an individualistic view for their own child's personal circumstances (Larner and Phillips, 1994). The vast majority of parents claimed that quality was a high priority for them when choosing childcare with 'word of mouth' being the main (but not always exclusive) method parents used to ascertain the quality of a setting. Practitioners appeared to agree with these findings but gave other sources of information regarding quality of provision more significance than the parents had acknowledged.

Do parents and practitioners have the same perception and/or understanding of quality?

This chapter has considered the perceptions of quality from a historical, practical, parental and practitioner viewpoint. There will continue to be ongoing debates as to what ensures quality provision with different voices being heard at different times, depending on political motivation and cultural drivers. Within this chapter an attempt has been made to draw these different perspectives together, considering the importance placed on quality by parents in their motivation for deciding on childcare. Although aware of the observable measures of quality, parents are consistent in their views that childcare also needs to meet their needs in terms of practical and flexible provision.

Practitioners also acknowledge the importance of this, especially as there is now a childcare marketplace. However they also seem to realise that quality practice is about meeting the needs of the children in their care, supporting their learning and development, nurturing their growth in confidence, self-esteem and celebrating their individual personalities. Alongside this an important aspect of quality is ensuring that *Every Child Matters* is addressed, the EYFS is implemented and health and safety maintained. Parents' views, practitioners' endeavours and the structural constraints of policy and legislation have some way to go before they reach common ground where quality practice can be easily defined – with the child at the centre of the process.

Summary

Writing the chapter has allowed me to reflect and think about the very nature of 'quality' in my own setting and within my own practice. This developed from engaging in a university programme of professional development. A challenging assignment late in the course provided a platform to articulate my views. However, the whole course was a vehicle for reflection. It made me more confident to express my views and more confident to challenge expert opinion. It has allowed me to consider what is really meant by quality and the differing perspectives that can be drawn into a debate about 'good practice' in early years childcare. It has also allowed me to challenge some of my preconceived ideas and the way the notion of quality and working in partnership with parents is sometimes imposed upon practitioners. The whole process has refined and developed my thinking and practice. I hope the views contained in this chapter may provide others with food for thought, both encouraging them to consider what we (in our own settings) perceive quality to be whilst also reminding those involved in their own and others' professional development of the distinct need to find ways to listen to those most closely involved, namely, parents.

Suggested further reading

- Flett, M. (2008) 'Developing quality early childhood programmes in United Kingdom', *Early Childhood Matters*, 110: 25–30.
  To achieve the best for young children it is necessary to adopt a different mindset on the way that quality provision is made. This article looks in depth at how the provision of early childhood in the United Kingdom has evolved over time and the direction in which efforts to improve quality have developed.

- Mooney, A. and Munton, A. (1998) 'Quality in early childhood services: parent, provider and policy perspectives', *Children and Society*, 12: 101–12.
  This paper describes a series of discussions on the meaning of quality in early childhood services. Parents, day-care providers and other stakeholders took part.

- Moss, P. and Pence, A. (eds) (1994) *Valuing Quality in Early Childhood Services: New Approaches to Defining Quality*. London: Paul Chapman Publishing.
  The book advocates that the process of defining quality should involve a range of stakeholder groups, including children, parents, staff, care providers, researchers, employers and the community. A key issue that emerges is the need for new and creative approaches to the development of an inclusionary process in the definitions and attainment of quality care.

References

Abbott, L. (1994) 'Introduction: the search for quality in the early years', in L. Abbott and R. Rodger (eds), *Quality Education in the Early Years*. Buckingham: Open University Press.

Baldock, P., Fitzgerald, D. and Kay, J. (2005) *Understanding Early Years Policy*. London: Paul Chapman Publishing.

Ball, C. (1994) *Start Right: The Importance of Early Learning*. London: Royal Society of Arts.

Brophy, J. and Statham, J. (1994) 'Measure for measure: values, quality and evaluation', in P. Moss and A. Pence (eds), *Valuing Quality in Early Childhood Services: New Approaches to Defining Quality*. London: Paul Chapman Publishing.

Ceglowski, D. (2004) 'How stake holder groups define quality in child care', *Early Childhood Education Journal*, 12(2): 101–10.

Committee for Economic Development (CED) (1993) 'Why child care matters: preparing young children for a more productive America'. http://www.ced.org/docs/report/report_childcare.pdf (accessed 29.09.2008).

Department for Children, Schools and Families (DCSF) (2006) *Raising Standards – Improving Outcomes: Statutory Guidance, Early Years Outcomes Duty, Childcare Act 2006*. Nottingham: DCSF.

Department for Children, Schools and Families (DCSF) (2008) *Statutory Framework for the Early Years Foundation Stage*. Nottingham: DCSF.

Department for Education and Skills (DfES) (2004) *Every Child Matters: Change for Children*. Nottingham: DfES.

Department of Education and Science (DES) (1990) *Starting with Quality: Report of the Committee of Enquiry into the Quality of Education Experience Offered to Three and Four Year Olds*. Rumbold Report. London: HMSO.

East Dunbartonshire Council (2006) 'Early Years and Childcare: East Dunbartonshire Council's Parent Survey 2006'. http://www.eastdunbarton.gov.uk/Web%20Site/Live/EDWebLive.nsf/40841fd2fca11fe280256a5b0047a5ff/d9cb3d6dd15ea15e80256e770056accc/$FILE/Early%20years%20parent%20survey.pdf (accessed 29.09.2008).

Fawcett, M. (2000) 'Early childhood care and education services in Britain', in M. Boushel, M. Fawcett and J. Selwyn (eds), *Focus on Early Childhood: Principles and Realities*. Oxford: Blackwell Science.

Flett, M. (2008) 'Developing quality early childhood programmes in United Kingdom', *Early Childhood Matters,* 110: 25–30.

Halle, T. and Vick, J. (2007) *Quality in Early Childhood Care and Education Settings: A Compendium of Measures*. Prepared by Child Trends for the Office of Planning, Research and Evaluation, Administration for Children and Families, U.S. Department of Health and Human Services. http://www. childtrends.org/Files//Child_Trends2007_12_10_FR_CompleteCompendium.pdf (accessed 20.07.2008).

Harms, T., Clifford, M. and Cryer, D. (1998) *Early Childhood Environment Rating Scale: Revised Edition (ECERS-R)*. Williston, VT: Teachers College Press.

Herefordshire County Council Early Years and Extended Services (HCCEYES) (2007) *Survey of Parental Demand for Childcare*. Hereford: Herefordshire County Council.

Herefordshire Early Years Development and Childcare Partnership (EYDCP) (2008) 'Deciding what's best for your child: a guide to education for four year olds'. http://www.education.herefordshire.gov.uk/DOCS/Deciding_Whats_Best.pdf (accessed 29.09.2008).

Katz, L. (1994) 'Perspectives on the quality of early childhood programmes', *Phi Delta Kappan,* 76(3): 200–5.

Kazimirski, A., Smith, R., Butt, S., Ireland, E. and Lloyd, E. (2008) 'National Centre for Social Research report: childcare and early years survey 2007: parents' use, views and experiences'. http://publications.dcsf.gov.uk/eOrderingDownload/DCSF-RR025.pdf (accessed 28.09.2008).

Larner, M. and Phillips, D. (1994) 'Defining and valuing quality as a parent', in P. Moss and A. Pence (eds), *Valuing Quality in Early Childhood Services: New Approaches to Defining Quality.* London: Paul Chapman Publishing.

Melhuish, E. (2003) 'A literature review of the impact of early years provision on young children with emphasis given to children from disadvantaged backgrounds'. http://www.nao.org.uk/publications/nao_reports/03-04/268_literaturereview.pdf (accessed 29.09.2008).

Mooney, A. and Munton, A. (1998) 'Quality in early childhood services: parent, provider and policy perspectives', *Children and Society,* 12: 101–12.

Mooney, A., Cameron, C., Candappa, M., McQuail, S., Moss, P. and Petrie, P. (2003) 'Early Years and Childcare International Evidence Project'. http://www.surestart.gov.uk/_doc/P0000820.doc (accessed 29.09.2008).

Moss, P. (1994) 'Defining quality: values, stakeholders and processes', in P. Moss and A. Pence (eds), *Valuing Quality in Early Childhood Services: New Approaches to Defining Quality.* London: Paul Chapman Publishing.

National Audit Office (NAO) (2004) *Early Years: Progress in Developing High Quality Childcare and Early Education Accessible to All.* London: HMSO.

National Quality Improvement Network (NQIN) (2007) *Quality Improvement Principles: A Framework for Local Authorities and National Organisations to Improve Quality Outcomes for Children and Young People.* London: National Children's Bureau.

Pascal, C. and Bertram, T. (1997) *Effective Early Learning: Case Studies in Improvement.* London: Hodder and Stoughton.

Peralta, M. (2008) 'Quality: children's right to appropriate and relevant education', *Early Childhood Matters,* 110: 3–12.

Pugh, G. (2006) 'The policy agenda for early childhood services', in G. Pugh and B. Duffy (eds), *Contemporary Issues in the Early Years.* London: Sage Publications.

Siraj-Blatchford, J. and MacLeod-Brudenell, I. (1999) *Supporting Science, Design and Technology in the Early Years.* Maidenhead: Open University Press.

Sylva, K., Mehuish, E., Sammons, P., Siraj-Blatchford, I. and Taggart, B. (2004) *The Effective Provision of Pre-School Education (EPPE) Project: Findings from Pre-school to end of Key Stage 1.* London: DfES.

Sylva, K., Siraj-Blatchford, I. and Taggart, B. (2003) *Assessing Quality in the Early Years: The Early Childhood Environment Rating Scale – Extension (ECERS-E): Four Curricular Subscales.* Stoke-on-Trent: Trentham Books.

Woodhead, M. (1996) 'In search of the rainbow: pathways to quality in large scale programmes for young disadvantaged children'. http://www.bernardvanleer.org/publication_store/publication_store_publications/in_search_of_the_rainbow_pathways_to_quality_in_large-scale_programmes_for_young_disadvantaged_children/file (accessed 30.09.2008).

13

From Experienced Practitioner to Reflective Professional

Sue Callan

Chapter objectives

Is reflecting on practice a valuable asset to have as a developing early years graduate? The answer might be an unequivocal yes, due to the valuable insights that this process gives to practice. However, getting to the point where it is possible to reflect positively on practice is no easy journey. This is especially so for someone entering higher education, because of the competing demands on their time and their studies. It is also because their studies are now influenced by changes to the qualifications framework throughout the UK – changes that have driven forward the need for practitioners to gain specific and relevant qualifications which requires them to navigate personal transitions through progressive continuing professional development (CPD). They are now expected to respond to national policies, be adept at working in partnership with parents and other professionals, engage in purposeful curriculum design, and consider their own practice and its impact on children and families; in effect to value, understand and reflect upon developing concepts of what might be called 'new professionalism' in the early years sector.

This chapter explores these issues in a picture of practice that has emerged from one Sector-Endorsed Foundation Degree in Early Years (SEFDEY) taught as an outreach programme in partnership between a university and a local authority Children's Workforce Development Team. It considers ways in which students have become consciously reflective professionals

(Continued)

(Continued)

and their transitions and learning journeys. Their experiences are articulated through 'student voices' alongside a commentary on the features of reflective practice represented. These contributions were captured as part of informal, longitudinal and qualitative research for ongoing critical reflection on practice in the same period (Callan, 2007, 2008). This personal process was in itself valuable as it showed a commitment to reflecting not only on the views of students, but on the shared experience gained by collaboration on a course of professional development developed through ongoing evaluation and responses to external pressures for change. It is hoped that the 'voices' of participants will have resonance with students following similar routes to qualifications and professional status within the sector.

The chapter highlights:

- the *existing* strengths of practitioners represented in SEFDEY programmes as the basis for positive professional development through the decision to participate in higher education;
- how reflection in practice can be represented through self-awareness arising from the emotional dimension of CPD;
- illustrating changing awareness and beliefs concerning 'knowledge' as represented in reflection.

Taking a picture of practice – getting the right images?

A simple way of describing the process of gathering information for this chapter would be to say, students following a foundation degree in early years have participated in the development of this chapter. However, it was a little more complex than this. It involved engaging with them in a discussion of their own professional development and their own perspectives on how this had altered and refined their thinking. Underpinning this approach were guiding principles drawn from the theoretical and philosophical values of critical theorists such as Horton and Freire (1990), who insist on situating educational activity in the lived experience of participants – enabling us to find a range of ways to explore practice. Their emphasis on respectful dialogue (rather than technical features of the curricula) develops new ways of explaining experience and acting in the world (consciousness-raising). For the critical theorists this transformational model of education leads to change – for SEFDEY students this is both personal and professional, directly transforming practice – but in the wider context action that is informed and linked to certain values and generates change for social justice and human development.

These views link directly to contemporary pedagogical principles. The Reggio Emilia philosophy (Malaguzzi, 1998) is based on a philosophy that respects the concept of a community of inquiry replicated here in the course community of practice. Within this model, there is a deliberate attempt to share power and expertise in the 'classroom'. This commitment to 'democratic classrooms' is intended to enable the personal growth of course participants, which is underpinned by a relational approach to teaching and learning also represented by the work of Carl Rogers (1983). The two converge in the phenomenological approach to qualitative research and use of personal narratives articulated by Van Manen (1997), and used to support earlier writing (Callan, 2007). These models are also applied to Brookfield's four lenses (1995) for developing critical reflective practice and the promotion of emotional literacy in the 'classroom' – through use of activities based on reflective writing approaches proposed by Bolton (2005) and Rainer (2004). Such an approach allows practitioners to realise that they know more than they think if reflective practice is represented in a meaningful context (represented by the work of Atkinson and Claxton, 2000, and Claxton, 1997). The picture of practice is also underpinned by a shared commitment in the team of professionals who teach on the course. They make a purposeful attempt to not let academic requirements intimidate or undermine progression of reflective qualities that will be of immediate benefit in the workplace. The importance of a gradual, supported introduction to study is acknowledged, as is allowing students time to grow and reflect in the programme. This is best articulated by a student who said:

> Before the SEFDEY I had not been in education for almost 14 years. I was very worried about my writing skills but as the course progressed I felt we were eased into the HE studying process. I felt we were fully supported (to succeed). It was also at that time I grew to be a reflective practitioner. I learnt more in that 2 and a half years than later in my BA Hons studying. (Summer 2008 response to a research activity, Foundation degree graduate autumn 2005, achieved BA (Hons) January 2008, currently EYPS candidate)

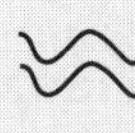

Point for reflection – there are pressures on course teams too

- Ask yourself, is there now a clear movement towards the 'qualified, reflective professional'?
- Are they now expected to be a leader in their field, able to multitask, understand the need for compassionate leadership, plan a month of activities in minutes, write reports in seconds, and complete essays at the drop of a hat?

(Continued)

(Continued)

The last question is a little 'tongue in cheek' but there is a developing expectation that it is possible to move students into the university sector and somehow give them these skills. There is also a traditional expectation in the university sector that students are established 'independent learners' and are intrinsically motivated to engage in professional development. However, for some students this is less a self-directed choice, but a response to external pressures and requirements, in a much wider social, cultural and political context. There is now a significant drive towards qualifications in early years contexts, therefore a challenge for a course team is not only to support the professional changes and expectations that abound, but the personal change that inevitably results. Moreover, there is a need to promote wider consciousness and reflection – because critical reflection is a recognised force for *change* – personal, professional and political. Therefore, course teams must be aware of the demands this makes of their time and energy. They are striving to make good practice accepted practice and promote training which is ethically appropriate for practice in a sector placed in the forefront of national policies for social justice and inclusion.

Caught in the middle: the student dilemma

Adult education is conventionally based on the notion of 'self actualisation' described by Maslow (1968) – the idea that individuals are striving towards achievement of potential as a natural process of lifespan development. Such a model certainly 'fits' with the expectation of learners in this context, however, for the experienced practitioners, this is far from the case (Callan, 2007). The comment below is an interesting view on the question who are the student practitioners in the midst of this clamour for change and whose CPD is continually formed by it?

> When I first started the course I felt an impostor, almost expecting someone asking me what I was doing here and ask me to leave. Worries about the amount of time I had spent out of the education system (35 years), led me to doubt whether I was capable ... I had the benefit of 20 years experience rising from helper in my setting to supervisor, but with no recent learning I felt disadvantaged (Spring 2008, end of level 4 reflective essay)

Indeed, the demographic characteristics of Foundation Degree Award (FDA) participants reported by the Quality Assurance Agency for Higher Education (QAAHE) review (2005) and a series of qualitative and quantitative DfES-sponsored research reports since 2003, including research for this chapter (Callan, 2007, 2008), represents enduring characteristics of the SEFDEY student cohort as:

- lacking confidence in ability across a range of study skills including ICT;
- having had little encouragement to have high academic or career expectations;
- mature students often torn between competing priorities for study and family life,
- feeling unsupported by peers in the workplace;
- having a negative personal self-image, which is reinforced by lack of status, pay and recognition in the workforce (lack of a professional 'voice').

What this tells us is that these personal negatives must be overcome in order to facilitate reflective practice and personal professional development. Therefore, introducing, explaining, and engaging with the notion of reflective practice must be a careful process. Previous experiences of learning may have encouraged an 'absolute' approach to knowledge as something finite, technocratic and skill based, with assessment based on finding 'right' answers – resulting in dependency on academic staff. Use of reflective techniques help identify the transition to other ways of 'knowing' and should enable a positive response to personal and professional change. It is crucial that course teams present reflection in terms of facilitating student transitions, rather than in a narrow academic domain where the practitioner is made to feel 'unworthy' or oppressed. In contrast, this next contribution indicates that through participation in the SEFDEY the student has made a journey towards being a *reflective professional* by challenging existing assumptions and ideas.

> Throughout my studies for the NNEB I was taught through the tutors own beliefs. Developing my own skills or sourcing independent research was not then encouraged. When I qualified I realised tutors aren't always correct. The SEFDEY has taught me to access information independently, making my own conclusions on good practice. (Autumn 2005, on graduating at level 5 final reflective essay)

New constructs: the reflective professional

Angela Nurse (2007) has analysed the changing concept of professionalism in society, noting that widening access to graduate-level training and qualification has extended 'professional status' to many job roles in the field of social care. This 'new' professionalism is defined by:

- high levels of educational attainment;
- self-motivated, ongoing professional and personal development, including training of others;
- working practice based upon an ethical approach drawn from historical, theoretical, ethical and philosophical traditions.

To this may be added the ability to reflect and challenge established ways of working; and to shed preconceived ideas and engage in study that allows and promotes reflection on theory and its links with practice (Reed, 2008). This would be consistent with the expectations placed on practitioners in the early childhood sector, although not necessarily the professional status afforded to the workforce – a theme consistent across reviews of student experience in the SEFDEY (Knight et al., 2006) and recent work by Cooke and Lawton (2008). Yet there is certainly evidence to suggest that the moral imperative articulated by students is based on qualities and attributes shown by Nurse (2007) to have strongly professional characteristics.

> My personal vision is to be acknowledged by parents, multi-disciplinary teams and agencies as a high quality, inclusive provision working in partnership with the local community to meet the needs of the children in our care, following a child-led approach to the curriculum. (December 2007, prior to graduating to level 6/EYPS route to BA (Hons), voluntary sector Pre-school Supervisor and Children's Centre Nursery Manager)

For this practitioner, professionalism is articulated as synonymous with quality – where quality is not only seen in terms of 'inspection quality' but the idea of knowing what is good quality because s/he has reflected on what this means. S/he has also demonstrated an awareness of accountability for practice, which Pound (2008) suggests is another indicator of professionalism. Indeed, students are often *already* accredited for 'professionalism' if status of sector quality schemes and inspection frameworks are recognised as indicators. For instance:

> Ofsted awarded my provision an outstanding grade. Working as an 'approved' network childminder, I aimed to progress further my professional development on to the 'accredited' status. This course has given me the strength, terminology and final commitment to reach the standard required as I have just been notified of my successful application. (Spring 2008, end of level 4 reflective essay)

Viewed from this perspective, the 'new professional' represented in this chapter is a particular phenomenon. S/he has not simply progressed through the various training routes, but consciously decided to engage in CPD whilst experiencing and *implementing in practice* the entire gamut of change. S/he is uniquely qualified to contribute to debates about the workforce and must be represented. Such practitioners are not simply created by policy initiatives and pilot schemes, but *made* as the result of lived experiences and a reflective process as advocated by Van Manen (1997) and Brookfield (1995). As such the participants are authentic representatives of workforce development and professional qualities identified by Moss (2006) in 're-envisioning' a workforce characterised by ethical and value-based reflective practice.

In considering issues of leadership and accountability as features of professionalism, Pound (2008) extends the aspects outlined by Nurse (2007). It should also be recognised that the assessment standards and judgements of EYPS candidates place emphasis on leading and supporting others in reflective practice (CWDC, 2006). It is evident from these few examples that definitions of professionalism include reflection and self-evaluation. In addition, the 'quality' schemes developed over time by Pascal and Bertram (1997) and the principles outlined by the National Quality Improvement Network (2007), all place emphasis on self-assessment and evaluation of practice based on *reflexivity*. Pound (2008: 54) clarifies this as standing back from practice to critically appraise perspectives, assumptions and judgements. The challenge for the SEFDEY course team in this context is to promote reflexivity in experienced practitioners as they negotiate the academic learning journey against a background of relentless change in the sector.

New constructs: representing reflection

New ideas about the nature of professionalism and the provision of training and qualification routes involving partnerships across further and higher education cultures require different perspectives and relationships for teaching and learning. The power-sharing dynamic in the classroom has previously been acknowledged, but this picture of practice also includes active participation in course management and delivery by local authority colleagues through the Workforce Development Team. Observing and participating in this partnership, in their more familiar roles as experienced practitioners, is fundamental to students' recognition of sector values in action as well as shared reflection across the agencies concerned. This enhances the effective local community of practice to which the course contributes.

The SEFDEY course team has made deliberate use of Brookfield's (1995) four lenses for critical reflection to support students' representations and awareness of these processes. This is used to demonstrate the key elements of 'reflection' in process, provides a rationale for all course activities and promotes continuity in transition to teaching at Honours level described in Chapter 1. The aspects of Brookfield's strategies also scaffold the course mentoring system (Robins, 2006), development of enhanced reading and research skills, use of learning journals, and creative representations of experience. These techniques for identifying the student response to the programme can also be aligned with the characteristics of the Mosaic approach to researching children's experience (Clark and Moss, 2001). More recently, the team has considered the use of questions such as those adapted from the work of Ryde (2007) who considers these as prompts when leading and managing.

Thinking about strengths

- Can I recognise things I did well?
- What am I most proud of?

Thinking about feelings

- How do I feel about what I have done?
- Were my instincts right?
- Did my actions support my values and beliefs?

Re-integrated thinking

- Were there more than one possible solution/action I could have taken?
- Can I identify their strengths and weaknesses?

Insight thinking

- What does this experience tell me?
- Can I learn from this?

Above and beyond thinking

- How would others view my actions?
- Would they see things differently?

The questions are a tangible means of reflecting on practice within a particular culture, context, or situation. Reflexivity is being able to see oneself clearly as an individual within these cultures, contexts or situations. It moves us towards what Bolton (2005) suggests when she considers not only reflective practice, but also reflexivity. This she illustrates as part of the dynamic between tutor and student working together, and suggests that students should formulate their own questions about the situations in which they find themselves (reflective) and the self they find there (reflexive). Moreover, she suggests that engaging in such reflection promotes a deeper understanding of actions that can lead to an improvement in professional practice. Such an approach forms a value-base for delivery of the course programme. The developing reflexivity of students is demonstrated by the ethical basis for practice reflected by notes from a small-scale study presented by a student:

> To achieve a truly inclusive and high quality practice it is vital that practitioners take heed of the views of all stakeholders, not just those who have the power to dictate standards. I am driven by a desire to be the best early years practitioner I can be and I recognise that building relationships and working collaboratively with parents is vital and necessary to achieve this. I am aware that as a practitioner and parent I have my own personal views and bias as to what constitutes quality in early years provision and this may affect my research both in how I conduct it and interpret my findings. (BA (Hons) 2008/2009 current student)

Point for reflection

Reflective practice has at its heart philosophical concepts and the views of countless researchers, and these have been discussed in Chapter 1 by Karen Appleby. This theoretical base forms the foundation for the development of reflective *practitioners* in touch with their own emotions and behavioural responses, familiar with the values and theoretical basis for work with children and families.

(Continued)

(Continued)

The whole taught programme is about journeys and reflection, development of skills and effectiveness in practice. The support of fellow students, tutors, critical friend, colleagues and family have helped me to cope with and successfully complete so far. I am now aware of my own abilities and strengths, more objective and evaluate more without finding fault with myself. I have become more confident and value myself as a professional. It has helped me develop as a person and benefited my whole life. (Spring 2008, on completion of level 4 semester one)

Although s/he may not yet be able to articulate philosophical theories, the practitioner is aware that knowledge represents ways of interpreting lived experience in the context of wider forces. S/he is ready to 'fly' as an independent constructor of her own knowledge and theories for practice. S/he is in fact developing strategies that can be said to build upon:

- the experience of change;
- personal choices to engage in challenging professional development in order to meet the requirements of workforce development in the sector in the same period;
- professionalism, most recently defined in analysis of early years practice, specifically reflexivity and leadership for change;
- finding academic language to articulate and reproduce a rationale for practice;
- engaging in critical reflection of the values and assumptions underpinning teaching and learning practice.

New constructs: developing communities of practice

There is a developing view that suggests that the community of experienced practitioners within the SEFDEY, will facilitate shared inquiry. Indeed, Chapter 10 by Victoria Cooper illustrates the need to engage with students and develop shared perspectives and rationales about learning. Within the programme used to illustrate this chapter the staff team have also been instrumental in introducing to this community the theories and principles, politics and cultural perspectives about which practitioners are less experienced. This is the driver towards enabling *critical* reflective – or *reflexive* – practice, which is distinguished by its outcome for change as described by Etherington (2004) and Pound (2008). This can be illustrated by the voices of those most closely involved:

- **Reflection on experience** – 'reflection is an important part of the working process in which professional practitioners re-visit strategies and teaching techniques in order to improve'. (December 2007, graduating practitioner level 5)
- '**Reflection in action** is the hawk in your mind constantly circling over your head watching and advising on your actions – while you are practising' Bolton (2005: 25). (Cited in level 5 student/practitioner reflective essay Autumn 2007)
- **Reflection on action** – 'I bring my whole self to my practice which can lead to vulnerability fearing failure because of the attitudes of others. I feel I have developed a basic confidence in being more able to take risk and see where that risk leads me ... and to trust my own instincts [example given]. The whole process was emotionally draining as it made me question my actions and reflect on my practice'. (December 2007, graduating practitioner level 5)

It can also be illustrated by a student who brings together the three components saying:

> This unit has shown me that I have more knowledge than I realised. I didn't learn a great deal, but I did gain greater understanding and with that understanding I feel more confident in myself. I firmly believe that intuition should not be dismissed. Being a reflective practitioner is nothing new, it is what we do all the time. (Summer 2006, reflective essay end of level 4 – Practitioner and NVQ assessor)

The student is identifying that s/he has been applying knowledge in action. Yet theory of reflective practice is not directly 'taught' in the course – this response is the result of the student's *own* reflection (transitional knowledge in beginning to form his/her own ideas). Towards the end of the degree programme some students are independently exploring theoretical reading and need to be able to discuss this with tutors, mentors and workplace colleagues in order to apply ideas in practice and prepare for graduate study at BA (Hons) level. The practical day-to-day result of these activities will see practitioners reporting greater risk taking, and recognition of professional *opportunities* in new challenges presented by the sector rather than a perception of personal threat from change and innovation.

> The modules made me think in a different way. [Knowledge] is about freeing the mind to reach one's potential. This injected new life into my nursery. The curriculum module made me realise how little I knew. It really made me look at my values, who I aligned myself with, who I believed in and why. It made me realise that although I had strong ideas about children being in charge of their own learning, I sometimes still behaved very much like a teacher. I changed the planning to reduce the number of adult led activities and this had an immediate effect on the staff who felt less pressured to get things done and gave them more time to observe children. (Autumn 2007, SEFDEY level 5 prior to progressing to BA (Hons))

In reporting self-development this student demonstrates critical reflective practice as defined here by Etherington (2004: 19):

> an ability to notice our responses to the world around us, other people and events, and to use that knowledge to inform our actions, communications and understandings. To be reflexive we need to be *aware* of our personal responses and to be able to make choices about how to use them. We also need to be aware of the personal, social and cultural contexts in which we live and work and to understand how these impact on the way we interpret our world. (Original emphasis)

Point for reflection

The words of one student:

> If we want an effective framework of CD [continuous development], we need to support self esteem – the CWDC and the University need to be aware of all the components of each practitioner's life, environment and culture. If we are looking at personalised learning – then we should model that throughout our practice for children and adults alike – we should be looking at adult schemas and adult learning styles – we should be looking at why people have come into the industry (which it is now becoming more and more). EYPS is a political means to an end – it ticks a box – but not on every level – in order to extend learning and to develop CPD – we need a profession that is recognised in fiscal and cultural terms. (Summer 2008, in response to a research question)

The speaker is asking for recognition that their efforts in engaging in professional development and gaining a recognised qualification be given the status it deserves. It can be argued that what is being seen on the ground (from tutors and students) is the emergence of a 'new professional'. They are questioning, reflective, sometimes

(Continued)

(Continued)

assertive, and certainly adept at dealing with change. They have been created in part by the drive towards government regulation of every facet of early years practice. This has led to a raft of qualifications, constructed and coordinated by a 'workforce council' who have implored practitioners to gain qualifications, including Foundation Degrees. Whether this is a desire to quantify and measure everything or a genuine desire to improve standards is yet to emerge. What is clear is that many of these courses have been designed, developed and have evolved by committed teams of professionals in higher and further education. They have certainly moved away from 'training by numbers' or somehow teaching 'technical childcare skills'. Instead they have started to develop the qualities required of 'new professionals' – professionals who can reflect on practice and challenge preconceived ideas.

Summary

In a short overview of practice, it is only possible to provide a simple illustration of the change that is occurring in the way that professionals are being prepared for the future. It has, however, allowed the voices of practice to articulate the way they have been allowed to reflect on practice. It has also perhaps continued the debate about the very nature of professional transitions and underlined the expectation that is now placed on early years professionals. More and more practitioners are required to reflect, consider and focus on the way they provide services to children and families. For the future, this is likely to continue.

Suggested further reading 

- Brookfield, S.D. (1995) *Becoming a Critically Reflective Teacher.* San Francisco, CA: Jossey-Bass.

  This text explores the 'lenses' of reflective practice – the world of the child (in work-based practice), personal responses to the experience of the practitioner, engagement with others (mentoring relationships) and practitioner research including expert opinion, theory and literature.

- Rainer, T. (2004) *The New Diary – How to Use a Journal for Self-Guidance and Expanded Creativity.* New York: Penguin.

  A rationale for the 'learning journal' as a means to self-awareness.

- Robins, A. (ed.) (2006) *Mentoring in the Early Years.* London: Sage Publications.

An extended rationale for practice in development of a Sector-Endorsed Foundation Degree in Early Years (SEFDEY).

- Stroobants, H., Chambers, P. and Clarke, B. (eds) (2007) *Reflective Journeys: A Fieldbook for Facilitating Life-Long Learning in Vocational Education and Training.* Rome: Leonardo da Vinci REFLECT Project.

  A valuable resource for course teams and students which contains accessible theory of reflective practice and a facilitative tool-kit.

References

Atkinson, T. and Claxton, G. (eds) (2000) *The Intuitive Practitioner. On the value of not always knowing what one is doing.* Maidenhead: Open University Press.

Bolton, G. (2005) *Reflective Practice: Writing and Professional Development.* 2nd edn. London: Sage Publications.

Brookfield, S.D. (1995) *Becoming a Critically Reflective Teacher.* San Francisco, CA: Jossey- Bass.

Callan, S. (2007) 'The Foundation Degree in Early Years: student perceptions of themselves as learners and the experiences that have contributed to this view. Can an exploration of these issues enhance reflective practice?'. Unpublished MA dissertation.

Callan, S. (2008) 'Ongoing research journal for investigation student experience. Beyond the Statement of Requirement: reflective practice and the continuing professional development of Foundation Degree "graduates"'. Unpublished.

Children's Workforce Development Council (CWDC) (2006) *Early Years Professional National Standards.* London: CWDC.

Clark, A. and Moss, P. (2001) *Listening to Young Children: The Mosaic Approach.* London: National Children's Bureau.

Claxton, G. (1997) *Hare Brain Tortoise Mind. Why Intelligence Increases When You Think Less.* London: Fourth Estate.

Cooke, G. and Lawton, K. (2008) *For Love or Money: Pay, Progression and Professionalisation in the 'Early Years' Workforce.* London: Institute for Public Policy Research.

Etherington, K. (2004) *Becoming a Reflexive Researcher. Using Our Selves in Research.* London: Jessica Kingsley.

Horton, M. and Freire, P. (1990) *We Make the Road by Walking: Conversations on Educational and Social Change.* Philadelphia, PA: Temple University Press.

Knight, T., Tennant, R., Dillon, L. and Weddell, E. (2006) *Evaluating the Early Years Sector Endorsed Foundation Degree: A Qualitative Study of Students' Views and Experiences.* Nottingham: DfES.

Malaguzzi, L. (1998) 'History, ideas and basic philosophy: an interview with Lella Gandini', in C. Edwards, L. Gandini and G. Forman (eds), *The Hundred Languages of Children: the Reggio Emilia Approach – Advance Reflections.* 2nd edn. London: JAI Press.

Maslow, A. (1968) *Towards a Psychology of Being.* New York: Van Nostrand.

Moss, P. (2006) 'Structures, understandings and discourses: possibilities for re-envisioning the early childhood worker', *Contemporary Issues in Early Childhood,* 7(1): 30–41.

National Quality Improvement Network (NQIN) (2007) *Quality Improvement Principles: A Framework for Local Authorities and National Organisations to Improve Quality Outcomes for Children and Young People.* London: National Children's Bureau.

Nurse, A. (ed.) (2007) *The New Early Years Professional: Dilemmas and Debates.* London: David Fulton.

Pascal, C. and Bertram, T. (1997) *Effective Early Learning: Case Studies in Improvement.* London: Hodder and Stoughton.

Pound, L. (2008) 'Exploring Leadership: roles and responsibilities of the early years professional', in A. Paige-Smith and A. Craft (eds), *Developing Reflective Practice in the Early Years.* Maidenhead: Open University Press.

Quality Assurance Agency for Higher Education (QAAHE) (2005) *Learning from Reviews of Foundation Degrees in England Carried Out in 2004–05: Sharing Good Practice.* Gloucester: QAAHE.

Rainer, T. (2004) *The New Diary – How to Use a Journal for Self-Guidance and Expanded Creativity.* New York: Penguin.

Reed, M. (2008) 'Professional development through reflective practice', in A. Paige-Smith and A. Craft (eds), *Developing Reflective Practice in the Early Years.* Maidenhead: Open University Press.

Robins, A. (ed.) (2006) *Mentoring in the Early Years.* London: Sage Publications.

Rogers, C. (1983) *Freedom to Learn for the 1980s.* Columbus, OH: Merrell.

Ryde, R. (2007) *Thought Leadership – Moving Hearts and Minds.* London: Palgrave Macmillan.

Van Manen, M. (1997) *Researching Lived Experience. Human Science for an Action Sensitive Pedagogy.* Ontario: The Althouse Press.

Conclusion

Michael Reed and Natalie Canning

We hope having delved into some of the chapters in this book it has helped you to think about your own practice, the importance of reflection and how you might share with others what you have found interesting, what you could relate to and what relates to the children you work with. One of the overarching themes of the book is change in terms of policy and practice. It is also about recognising and to an extent celebrating sound professional practice and providing pictures of practice which illustrate the world of the early years professional. We hope that you will identify with some of the situations the new early years professional is faced with and that you have been able to reflect on how you have felt and reacted in those situations. Another main theme is reflection, which at a time of quick moving policy and practice, is important for all practitioners. In times of change we need to stop and reflect on the importance of placing the child at the centre of what we do and why we do it. Taking such a stance means we are on the way to valuing our profession and the most important aspect within it.

Within the collection of chapters clear themes for reflecting on practice emerge. The importance you place on your values in developing your professional practice and working for the best possible outcome for children resonate throughout all of the chapters. The importance of new legislation and understanding and applying new curricular developments has been an underpinning theme for all the chapters, however, the book also has another message about understanding your own values and those of others around you. It is about sharing your views and opinions and opening a dialogue not just with your colleagues but other practitioners you have contact with. This may be in a professional capacity, through informal networks, regional debates, national consultation or learning communities that you belong to. It is about sharing your knowledge and understanding, demonstrating your passion and reflecting on other people's views. We also hope that the chapters have broadened your views of some aspects of practice. They may have sparked an interest for you to investigate further and will inform your practice and help form who you are and where you come from as an early years practitioner. The aim has always been to contribute to building firm foundations of knowledge, values and practice in order to support the development of collegial, coherent and creative early years professionals.

The book not only provides an insight into the different ways in which reflective practice manifests itself in different early years contexts but also how reflective thinking provides dispositions towards learning, values and developing professional identity. The four sections of the book are loosely based on the four principles of the Early Years Foundation Stage, but demonstrate the importance of not only recognising the needs of the child, but also your needs in developing communities of practice which are reflective and collaborative. The chapters bring together not only research based on examples of reflection, but demonstrate that reflection is a key element to any early years practitioner, from nursery assistant to children's centre manager, and can be applied in any context. For you, reflective practice may be something that you already have developed skills in using in the context of your own professional development and in practice. For others this might be your first encounter with the concept. Whatever level of experience you have as an early years professional, we hope that you have been able to recognise the importance of being part of a community of practice where reflection is shared and sustained amongst the people most closely involved. We believe that reflective practice is a crucial part of what you do and understanding why you do it and will provide you with a platform for future development of practice and skills which you will be able to share not only with your colleagues, but with parents, your wider community, other professionals you work with and, most importantly, the children in your care. We wish you well on your learning journey which may present you with challenges along the way, but will ultimately provide you with a rich and stimulating starting point for any project you undertake, or initiative you become involved with. Reflective practice is the key to your early years future.

Useful Websites

The list is not presented as a definitive review of websites relating to reflective practice, but contains selected sites that we think are useful. We acknowledge that the Internet is a fast-moving part of our lives and websites often change or are adapted in some way. Therefore, the sites shown below are as up to date as possible but may be subject to change as time moves on.

British Library

www.bl.uk/welfarereform/issue61/childwuk.html
Useful weblink to the British Library which gives you updates on social welfare and childcare.

Bromley Childminding Association

www.bromleycma.org.uk/policies/policies_and_procedures.html
This website gives you examples of policies for childminders and is useful to all practitioners.

C4EO

www.c4eo.org.uk/default.aspx
A site that identifies and coordinates local, regional and national evidence of 'what works' to create a single and comprehensive picture of effective practice in delivering children's services. You can sign up for emailed updates.

Children's Plan

www.dcsf.gov.uk/publications/childrensplan/
A primary link to the Children's Plan and updates.

http://www.dcsf.gov.uk/publications/childrensplan/downloads/implementation_pack_summary.pdf
A summary of the Children's Plan Implementation Pack.

Children's Workforce and Development Council

www.cwdcouncil.org.uk/
An essential link to policy and practice for the early years workforce.

Children and Young People Now

www.cypnow.co.uk/myCYPNow/
This website allows you to sign up for emailed news and legislation updates.

Commission for Racial Equality

www.cre.gov.uk
Produces and fact files relating to employment and ethnicity.

Common Assessment Framework

www.everychildmatters.gov.uk/deliveringservices/caf/
The primary link to the CAF framework.

Department of Health

www.dh.gov.uk
Find the 'statistics' link for information on health care, workforce, public health, social care and links to the 'information centre' for health and social care.

Department of Health and Social Services

www.dhsspsni.gov.uk/index/hss/svg/svg-faq.htm
This site considers public safety and safeguarding vulnerable groups. It provides useful procedures, legislation and fact sheets.

Department for Trade and Industry

www.dti.gov.uk/employment/researchevaluation/index.html
Employment Market Analysis and Research which conducts periodic socio-economic benchmark surveys.

Department of Work and Pensions

www.dwp.gov.uk

You can find statistical reports produced by the Information and Analysis Directorate (IAD) on this website by clicking on the 'Resource Centre' link, at the top right-hand corner of the home page.

Early Years Foundation Stage

www.standards.dcsf.gov.uk/eyfs/
A useful link to the EYFS in detail.

***Every Child Matters*: and the Common Core of Skills and Knowledge**

www.everychildmatters.gov.uk
An important website to bookmark and return to on a regular basis, it contains essential information about policy and developments for those involved in early years practice.

Every Child Matters Outcomes Framework showing relevant indicators from the National Indicator Set

http://www.dfes.gov.uk/publications/childrensplan/downloads/ECM%20outcomes%20framework.pdf
A useful representation to view outcomes and see the policy developments related to ECM at a glance.

Home Office Equality Unit

www.homeoffice.gov.uk/equality-diversity/
This site relates to the Home Office responsibilities such as crime, the justice system and immigration via the 'Science, Research and Statistics' link.

Institute of Public Policy and Research

www.ippr.org
Here you will find a most useful document examining roles, responsibilities and conditions for early years practitioners.

National Children's Bureau

www.ncb.org.uk/dotpdf/open_access_2/earlyyears_timeline_20080228.pdf
A timeline detailing the policy directives and legislation in England, plus a list of websites and links to help with policy planning and updating legislation (some allow you to sign up for free regular updates via email).

National Statistics

www.statistics.gov.uk
A significant range of statistics including employment rates, retail sales, population and health statistics.

Ofsted

www.ofsted.gov.uk
Updates, policy and reports from Ofsted.

Powys

http://foundationphase.powys.gov.uk/index.php?p=7&c=1
The local authority website – useful information and examples of policies.

Scottish Government
www.scotland.gov.uk
Information about 'The Early Years Framework' (2008), The Scottish Government, St Andrew's House, Edinburgh.

Statutory Framework for the EYFS

http://www.standards.dfes.gov.uk/eyfs/resources/downloads/statutory-framework-update.pdf
A useful link to the EYFS statutory requirements in detail.

Sure Start

www.surestart.gov.uk
Follow the Special Educational Needs and Disability page for information on the funding for inclusion and information on the role of SENCOs.

The Standards Site

www.standards.dfes.gov.uk/eyfs/site/requirements/index.htm
A comprehensive site that contains specific links for early years (EYFS) providers and details of the legislation and regulations that providers should be aware of.

Teachers TV

http://www.teachers.tv/video/24245
Teachers TV provides you with EYFS video clips, interactive exercises, comments and news. You can sign up for emailed updates.

Index

Added to a page number 'f' denotes a figure and 't' denotes a table.